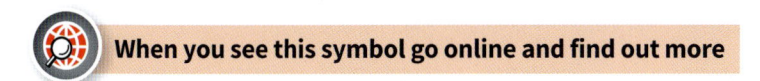

When you see this symbol go online and find out more

HARMONIZE 2
STUDENT BOOK

A2

Daniel Brayshaw

OXFORD
UNIVERSITY PRESS

			Vocabulary	Grammar	Reading
	Welcome p4 Video How to do project work About the projects		• Sports • Free-time activities • In a town • Animals • Animal body parts • Food • Question words • like + -ing / noun • Quantifiers • Present simple • Present continuous • Present continuous: future arrangements • Possessive pronouns		
1	**Then and now** p8 Video Opening a time capsule		• Verbs and their opposites • Adjectives for feelings	• Past simple: regular and irregular verbs • Past simple: (there) was / were	Blog: The birth of teenage culture Skill UP! Reading for gist
	PROJECT Create a time capsule	→	Project Builder 1 p9 →	Project Builder 2 p11 →	
2	**Art and design** p20 Video Today we're doing art		• Adjectives and synonyms • Materials	• Past continuous • Past continuous and past simple	Article: You know the picture, but did you know … ? Skill UP! Focus on the most important words when reading
	PROJECT Create an art and design gallery	→	Project Builder 1 p21 →	Project Builder 2 p23 →	
3	**Fresh air** p32 Video Designing a park		• Outdoor activities • Outdoor events	• will / won't for predictions • First conditional	Leaflet: Teens for greener cities (TGC) Skill UP! Using your own knowledge to help you understand a text
	PROJECT Design a park	→	Project Builder 1 p33 →	Project Builder 2 p35 →	
4	**A helping hand** p44 Video A day for doing good		• Personality adjectives • Phrasal verbs	• be going to for future plans and intentions • be going to and will for predictions	Article: Four things you can donate to charity Skill UP! Guessing the meaning of unknown words
	PROJECT Record or film a radio interview	→	Project Builder 1 p45 →	Project Builder 2 p47 →	
5	**Let's play** p56 Video Welcome to the games club!		• Senses • Gaming verbs	• can / can't, could / couldn't • Comparative and superlative adverbs	Blog: Memory Skill UP! Using pronouns
	PROJECT Make a set of games and challenges	→	Project Builder 1 p57 →	Project Builder 2 p59 →	
6	**Move it!** p68 Video Good morning?		• Exercise and the body • Personal hygiene	• Present perfect • Present perfect with ever and never	Article: Dump the junk! Skill UP! Using your own language to understand English
	PROJECT Create a health and fitness infographic	→	Project Builder 1 p69 →	Project Builder 2 p71 →	
7	**Skills for life** p80 Video How to learn with the internet		• Verbs and their noun forms • Verbs	• should / shouldn't, must / mustn't • have (got) to + infinitive without to	Article: You don't have to be an adult to be the best! Skill UP! Scanning
	PROJECT Create a how-to video	→	Project Builder 1 p81 →	Project Builder 2 p83 →	
8	**What a year!** p92 Video Looking at our yearbooks		• Things to do during the summer holidays • Jobs	• Reflexive and indefinite pronouns • Question tags	Online text chat: And the award goes to … Skill UP! Recognizing informal style
	PROJECT Create a group yearbook	→	Project Builder 1 p93 →	Project Builder 2 p95 →	

My grammar reference & practice p104–121   **Culture 360°** p122–126   **Irregular verb list** p127–128

Listening	Speaking	Writing	PROJECT
Short oral histories: Creepy places! **Skill UP!** Using pictures and labels to predict vocabulary	▶Video **Making and responding to suggestions** **Skill UP!** Showing interest during conversations	**A personal message** **Skill UP!** Using linkers	**Create a time capsule** p18 **Project skills:** Deciding together ▶ **Project coach:** Choosing ideas for your project
Project Builder 3 p13 →	Project Builder 4 p15 →	Project Builder 5 p17 →	
Podcast: Looks good, works well **Skill UP!** Listening for context	▶Video **Describing a photo or scene** **Skill UP!** Explaining unknown words	**An illustrated story** **Skill UP!** Making your illustrated story fun to read	**Create an art and design gallery** p30 **Project skills:** Planning and creating your display together ▶ **Project coach:** Creating a project planner
Project Builder 3 p25 →	Project Builder 4 p27 →	Project Builder 5 p29 →	
▶Video **Outdoor events** Video focus: Round-up videos	▶Video **Asking for and offering help** **Skill UP!** Showing that you are happy to help	**A speech** **Skill UP!** Writing a speech	**Design a park for the whole community** p42 **Project skills:** Giving a group speech or presentation ▶ **Project coach:** Using body language in presentations
Project Builder 3 p37 →	Project Builder 4 p39 →	Project Builder 5 p41 →	
▶Video **Feeling good about doing good** Video focus: Joining video calls	▶Video **Asking for, giving and reacting to advice** **Skill UP!** Using phrases that give you time to think	**A formal email** **Skill UP!** Writing a formal email, letter or message	**Record or film a radio interview about helping others** p54 **Project skills:** Practising in groups ▶ **Project coach:** Using your voice in recordings and videos
Project Builder 3 p49 →	Project Builder 4 p51 →	Project Builder 5 p53 →	
Vox pop: Gaming **Skill UP!** Listening for examples	▶Video **Interacting during games and activities** **Skill UP!** Asking, explaining or checking something during a game	**An online advert** **Skill UP!** Writing an online advert	**Make a set of games and challenges** p66 **Project skills:** Writing instructions ▶ **Project coach:** Giving feedback to other groups
Project Builder 3 p61 →	Project Builder 4 p63 →	Project Builder 5 p65 →	
Radio programme: Personal hygiene **Skill UP!** Listening for detail	▶Video **Talking about health problems** **Skill UP!** Expressing sympathy	**A survey report** **Skill UP!** Writing a survey report	**Create a health and fitness infographic** p78 **Project skills:** Dealing with disagreements ▶ **Project coach:** Using font and colour in infographics
Project Builder 3 p73 →	Project Builder 4 p75 →	Project Builder 5 p77 →	
▶Video **Sharing skills** Video focus: Using on-screen text in videos	▶Video **Giving spoken instructions** **Skill UP!** Using intonation when giving instructions	**Instructions and cue cards** **Skill UP!** Writing cue cards	**Create a how-to video** p90 **Project skills:** Teamwork and skills ▶ **Project coach:** Editing videos
Project Builder 3 p85 →	Project Builder 4 p87 →	Project Builder 5 p89 →	
▶Video **Dream jobs** Video focus: Asking the viewers questions in videos	▶Video **Expressing and responding to thanks** **Skill UP!** Responding to thanks with *Thank YOU*	**A reflective essay** **Skill UP!** Writing a reflective essay	**Create a group yearbook** p102 **Project skills:** Thinking about design ▶ **Project coach:** Creating a project design
Project Builder 3 p97 →	Project Builder 4 p99 →	Project Builder 5 p101 →	

Welcome

LESSON OBJECTIVES • Revise grammar and vocabulary

1 💬 Can you think of any examples of labyrinths in films, books, or public places?

2 💬 Read the instructions for *Labyrinth*. Then play the game in pairs or two teams.

INSTRUCTIONS

To play:
- Put your counters on 'START HERE'.
- Take turns to throw the dice and move 1–3 spaces:

  ⚀ or ⚁ = move 1 space
  ⚂ or ⚃ = move 2 spaces
  ⚄ or ⚅ = move 3 spaces

When you land on these spaces:

❓ Answer a vocabulary question. Move two more spaces for a correct answer.

❓ Answer a grammar question. Move two more spaces for a correct answer.

🗝 Collect a key.

🙋 Miss a turn.

👊 Move two more spaces (down only ▼)

🐴 Collect a horse. Move one extra space for the rest of the game.

Important: Answer the questions in order and don't answer the same question as the other team. Keep moving in your turn until you stop, e.g. land on an empty space. You can answer more than one question in the same turn.

To win:
- Collect one A and one B key from around the board.
- When you have two keys, go to the treasure. Land on an orange space to win.

3 Think about the game. Which questions are easy? Which are difficult? For more practice, go to page 104 and do the exercises.

CHECK IT! ➡ MY GRAMMAR REFERENCE & PRACTICE p104

VOCABULARY
Sports   Animals
Free-time activities Animal body parts
In a town   Food

GRAMMAR
Question words   Present continuous
like + -ing / noun   Present continuous:
Quantifiers   future arrangements
Present simple   Possessive pronouns

Complete the sentences with a word.
1 My friends and I _____ athletics.
2 What do you _____ photos of?
3 You can borrow a book from the _____.
4 People _____ surfing on these beaches.
5 The animal with the longest neck in the world is the _____.
6 You can catch a bus to the city centre from the bus _____ on London Road.
7 We went on every rollercoaster at the _____. They were so exciting!
8 Animals use their _____ to walk.

Choose the correct option.
9 Which of these foods is different to the others?
   bananas / **oranges** / **salmon** / **grapes**
10 **Sharks** / **Monkeys** / **Ants** live in the sea.
11 Birds use their **teeth** / **wings** / **tongues** to fly.
12 We **do** / **play** / **listen** video games at the weekend.
13 Can you make it sweeter with some **salt** / **eggs** / **sugar**?
14 Which of these animals can't fly?
    bees / **eagles** / **spiders**
15 Which of these is not made from milk?
    yoghurt / **cheese** / **pasta** / **ice cream**
16 Lena **did** / **played** / **went** judo for the first time last week.

Labyrinth

Complete the sentences with a word.
1 '_____ do you get to school every day?' 'By bus.'
2 _____ T-shirt do you like the best? The pink T-shirt or the yellow T-shirt?
3 Alicia is unhappy because she doesn't like _____ shopping.
4 There isn't _____ money left, but there is enough to buy some chocolate.
5 '_____ is Lewis going home early?' 'Because he's not feeling well.'
6 We haven't got _____ chairs for everyone. There are ten people and only eight chairs.
7 My sister _____ to rock music every day.
8 Sorry, I can't talk now. I'm _____ a film in the cinema.

Choose the correct option.
9 Marcus and Lucia like **playing** / **play** / **plays** tennis together.
10 We've got milk, but we haven't got **many** / **much** cheese.
11 My mum **works** / **working** in a large office.
12 I can't meet my friends this weekend because I **study** / **'m studying** for an exam.
13 'Is that Tom and Nina's dog?' 'Yes, I think it's **them** / **their** / **theirs**.'
14 My little brother never **do** / **does** / **is doing** arts and crafts at home.
15 What time are we **leave** / **leaves** / **leaving** tomorrow?
16 'Is that Leo's bike?' 'No, it isn't. It's **me** / **my** / **mine**.'

PROJECTS

LESSON OBJECTIVES • Find out about the course • Learn how to do project work

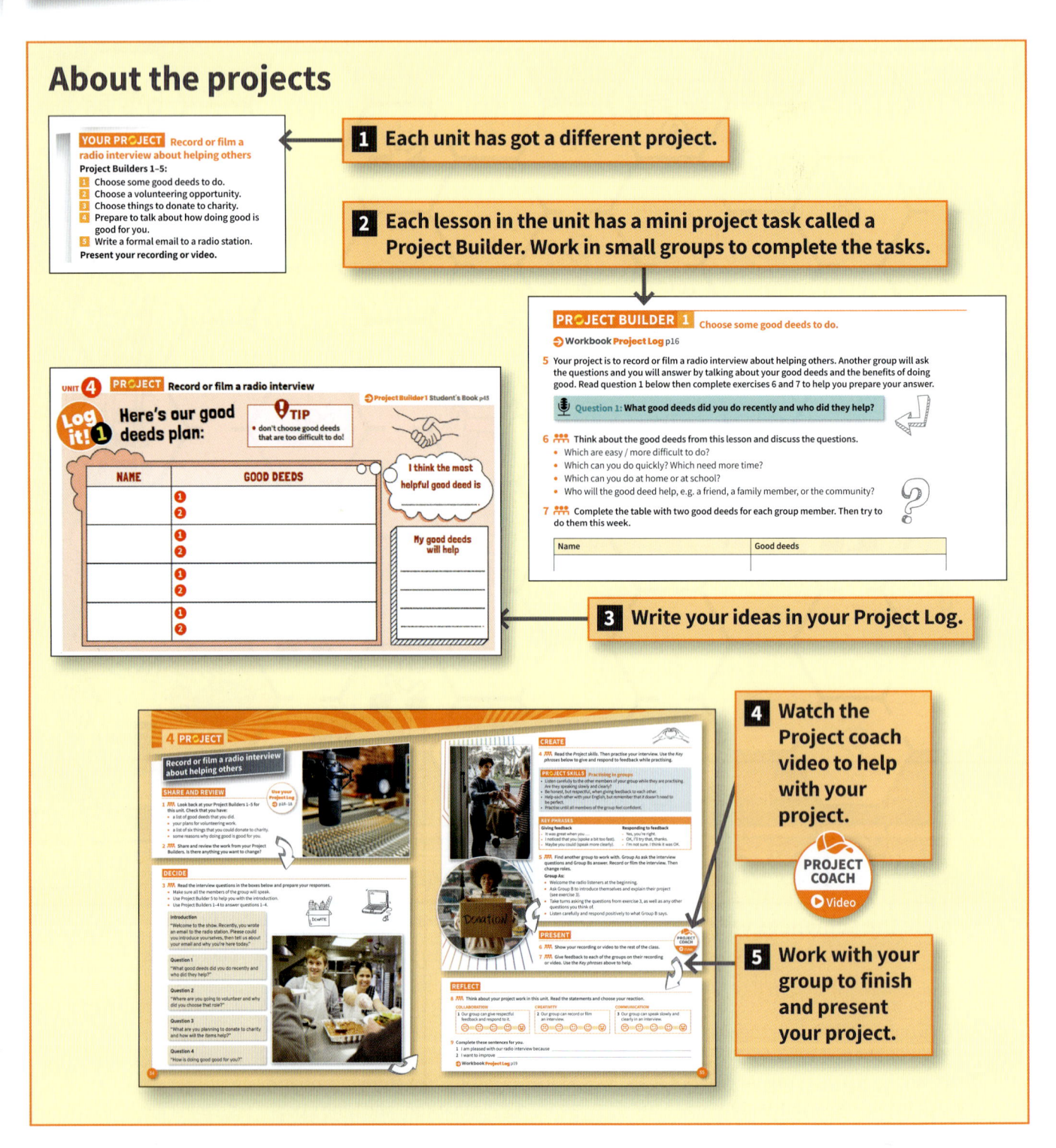

About the projects

YOUR PROJECT Record or film a radio interview about helping others

Project Builders 1–5:
1 Choose some good deeds to do.
2 Choose a volunteering opportunity.
3 Choose things to donate to charity.
4 Prepare to talk about how doing good is good for you.
5 Write a formal email to a radio station.

Present your recording or video.

1 Each unit has got a different project.

2 Each lesson in the unit has a mini project task called a Project Builder. Work in small groups to complete the tasks.

PROJECT BUILDER 1 Choose some good deeds to do.
Workbook Project Log p16

5 Your project is to record or film a radio interview about helping others. Another group will ask the questions and you will answer by talking about your good deeds and the benefits of doing good. Read question 1 below then complete exercises 6 and 7 to help you prepare your answer.

Question 1: What good deeds did you do recently and who did they help?

6 Think about the good deeds from this lesson and discuss the questions.
• Which are easy / more difficult to do?
• Which can you do quickly? Which need more time?
• Which can you do at home or at school?
• Who will the good deed help, e.g. a friend, a family member, or the community?

7 Complete the table with two good deeds for each group member. Then try to do them this week.

Name	Good deeds

3 Write your ideas in your Project Log.

4 Watch the Project coach video to help with your project.

5 Work with your group to finish and present your project.

---

1 Use *About the projects* and your books to answer the questions.

1 Look at page 8 of Unit 1 in your Student Book. What is the project in this unit?

2 How many Project Builders are there in each unit?
3 Where is the Project Log?
4 How many Project Log pages are there for each project?

2 💬 Do the quick quiz.

QUICK QUIZ

Find the units with these Project Builders in your Student Book.

- You design and describe a piece of street art. 2
- You create a wordsearch puzzle. ____
- You plan the events for a park's opening weekend. ____
- You write a formal email to a radio station. ____
- You prepare information for a yearbook section about future jobs. ____
- You make a list of possible topics for a how-to video. ____
- You choose items to include in a time capsule. ____
- You prepare a *Fitness* section for an infographic. ____

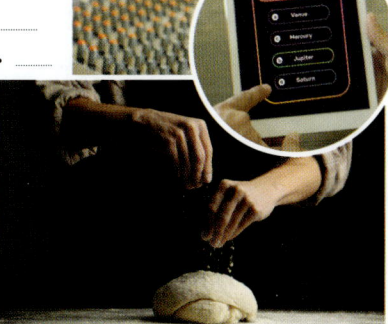

3 Read the *Project skills*. What can happen if you don't follow this advice?

PROJECT SKILLS Sharing work
- Share the work. Don't let one or two people do everything.
- If it's a big task or you need help, work with another person.

4 👥 Read the *Your Project* task. Imagine you are doing this project. Choose roles for each person in your group. Use the *Key phrases*.

KEY PHRASES
Planning
- We need to (design a poster).
- (Tom), why don't you (find photos online)?
- I can (write the presentation).
- Can you help me, (Sara)?

5 👥 Review your decisions. Did you share the work equally?

HOW TO DO PROJECT WORK

6 ▶ Video Watch the video about project work and answer the questions.
1. Look at the seven types of project at 0.20. Which of these types of project are in your Student Book?
2. Go to 4.31. Which of these tips for project work is the most difficult for you to do?
3. Can you think of other tips for project work?

Your Project
Project: Design and present a poster
Aim: Get more school students to recycle
Tasks:
- Design the poster
- Find photos online for the poster
- Do research online about other schools' recycling projects
- Write the presentation
- Practise and give the presentation

1 Then and now

UNIT OBJECTIVES

YOUR PROJECT Create a time capsule

Project Builders 1–5:
1. Write a note for the people who find your time capsule.
2. Choose items to include in your time capsule.
3. Complete a personal profile.
4. Write a description of an interesting place.
5. Write a personal message.

Present some of the items from your time capsule.

VOCABULARY
- Verbs and their opposites
- Adjectives for feelings

GRAMMAR
- Past simple: regular and irregular verbs
- Past simple: (there) was / were; past time phrases

LESSON OBJECTIVES
- Talk about ways to learn about the past
- Learn vocabulary related to time capsules

WARM-UP

1 Look at photos 1–3. Match them with A–C.
A ___ the ruins of an ancient city   B ___ a dinosaur fossil   C ___ an Egyptian tomb

2 💬 Discuss the questions.
1 What can people learn from the things in photos 1–3?
2 How can people learn about the past from TV, the internet, books, or other people?

3 ▶ Video Watch Curtis's vlog. What is a time capsule?

4 ▶ Video Watch again. Then answer the questions.
1 What is Curtis's main point about history?
2 What does Curtis say about dinosaur fossils?
3 How old is Angkor Wat, in Cambodia?
4 What did Howard Carter find?
5 Who made the time capsule and when?
6 Why did they make the time capsule?

Curtis's VLOG
Opening a time capsule

5 Complete the instructions with the words in the box.

| close   container   hide   include   inside   items   outside   safe |

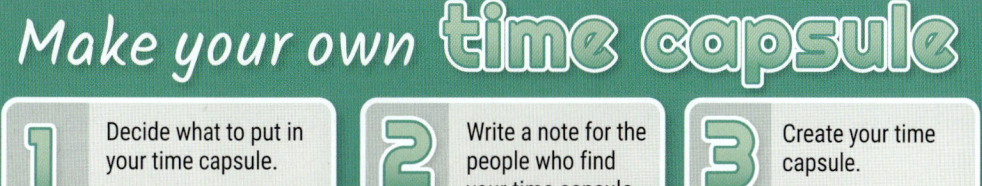

Make your own time capsule

1 Decide what to put in your time capsule. Collect ¹_____ and photos to help people understand what life is like in the present day.

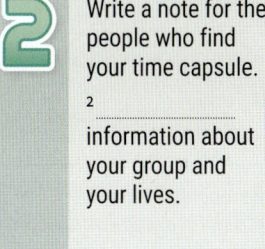

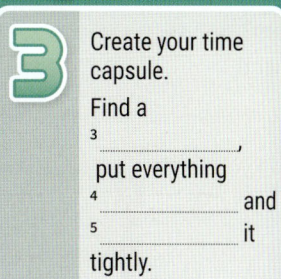

2 Write a note for the people who find your time capsule. ²_____ information about your group and your lives.

3 Create your time capsule. Find a ³_____, put everything ⁴_____ and ⁵_____ it tightly.

4 ⁶_____ your time capsule. Store it in a ⁷_____ place, for example, in a cupboard. Write the date that you want people to open it on the ⁸_____ of your time capsule.

6 💬 **MEDIATION** A friend doesn't speak English. With your partner, explain how to make a time capsule in your own language.

PROJECT BUILDER 1   Write a note for the people who find your time capsule.

➔ Workbook **Project Log** p4

7 👥 Decide what basic information about your group to put in a note for your time capsule.

> We need to give our names and ages, of course.

8 👥 Write your note.
To the people that find our time capsule, …

9

1.2 90s TIME CAPSULE

LESSON OBJECTIVES
- Learn what life was like for young people in the 1990s
- Talk about the past using regular and irregular verbs

VOCABULARY

1. 💬 What did Curtis and Amanda find inside the time capsule from 1999? Name the items in the pictures.
   They found some CDs ...

2. 💬 Read labels A–F and answer the questions in bold from the students of 1999.

3. Read the labels again and find the opposites of the verbs in the box. Which are in the past tense?

buy	disagree	disappear	disconnect
lend	lose	send	spend

   ✓ 'Borrow' means to take something *from* another person, knowing you will give it back. 'Lend' means to give something *to* another person, knowing they will give it back.

4. 💬 Complete the questions with the correct form of some of the verbs from exercise 3, including the opposites. Then ask and answer.
   1. Do you ever .... books from a library?
   2. Where do you usually .... clothes?
   3. Do you ever send or .... letters or postcards? Who to or from?
   4. How many devices do you and your family own that .... to the internet?
   5. Which bands and singers do you know that regularly .... awards?
   6. What do teenagers usually .... their money on?
   7. 'People today spend too much time looking at phones or computers.' Do you .... or disagree?
   8. What popular fashion or technology from today do you think will .... during the next ten years?

A The internet became popular in the 1990s. Now we can connect computers to the World Wide Web and share information. **Do computers look the same in your time?**

B Mobile phones are quite common now. You can receive messages and calls anywhere! **Do a lot of people have mobile phones in your time?**

C U2, the Spice Girls, Blur, Oasis – these bands sold millions of CDs and won many awards in the 1990s. **Are these bands still popular?**

D We watch films on VHS video tapes or DVDs. We borrow them from local rental shops. **Do you still use these?**

E Most of us agreed that the Nintendo Game Boy is the coolest device of the 1990s. A few students didn't agree, and voted for the Sega Game Gear instead. Anyway, both are great video games machines. You can take them everywhere! **Do your games machines look like the Game Boy?**

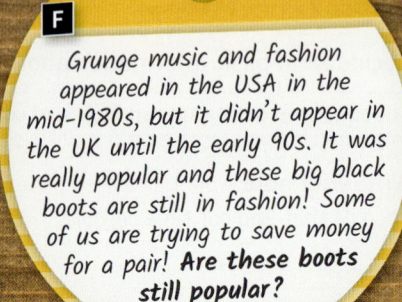

F Grunge music and fashion appeared in the USA in the mid-1980s, but it didn't appear in the UK until the early 90s. It was really popular and these big black boots are still in fashion! Some of us are trying to save money for a pair! **Are these boots still popular?**

GRAMMAR
Past simple: regular and irregular verbs

5 Complete the table about the past simple. Use the time capsule labels to help you.

		Affirmative	Negative
Regular verbs	I / He / She / It / We / You / They	agreed appeared saved	1 _____ 2 _____ didn't save
Irregular verbs	I / He / She / It / We / You / They	3 _____ spent 4 _____	didn't sell didn't spend didn't win
Questions and answers			
When did grunge appear?		It appeared in the 80s.	
Did you agree?		Yes, I did. / No, I didn't.	

CHECK IT! → MY GRAMMAR REFERENCE & PRACTICE p106

6 Complete the sentences with the past simple forms of the verbs in brackets.
1. Nintendo, the Japanese electronics company, _created_ (create) the Game Boy™. They _sold_ (sell) almost 120 million of them between 1989 and 2003.
2. Grunge fashion _____ (appear) at the same time as grunge music when bands like Nirvana and Pearl Jam became popular. It _____ (make) these boots fashionable again.
3. In the early 90s, CDs _____ (replace) cassettes as the most popular way to buy music.
4. Local rental shops _____ (be) everywhere. People _____ (not need to) travel very far to get a film to watch.
5. Mobile phones made calls and _____ (send) text messages, but they _____ (not connect) to the internet.
6. The first website _____ (go) online in late 1990. The first online shopping site _____ (open) in 1994. The first YouTube™ video _____ (not appear) until 2005 – it's called 'Me at the zoo'.

7 Match 1–6 in exercise 6 to labels A–F from the time capsule on page 10.

8 Write questions about the 1990s. Use the past simple.
1. How many / Game Boys / Nintendo sell?
2. What kind of music / Nirvana and Pearl Jam / play?
3. How / most people / listen to music in the 1990s?
4. Where / people / borrow films from in the 1990s?
5. Mobile phones / connect to the internet / in the 1990s?
6. When / the first website / go online?

9 Answer the questions from exercise 8 using the information from exercise 6.

10 **THINK** In what ways were 1990s entertainment and communication different to the present day?
> People didn't have smartphones or social media …

11 Ask questions about your partner's life when they were 8–10 years old.
> Did you have a pet when you were 8?
>> Yes, I did. I had a dog. And you?

1. have / pet?
2. What / sports / do?
3. What / films / like?
4. Where / spend / holidays?

PROJECT BUILDER 2

Choose items to include in your time capsule.

→ Workbook **Project Log** p4

12 Choose five items for your time capsule that show what life is like in the present day. Write notes about each of them. Use the mind map to help you.
Technology – Netflix™
- Netflix first appeared in the late 90s as an online DVD rental company – they lent DVDs to customers by post. But in 2007, the company started streaming films online.

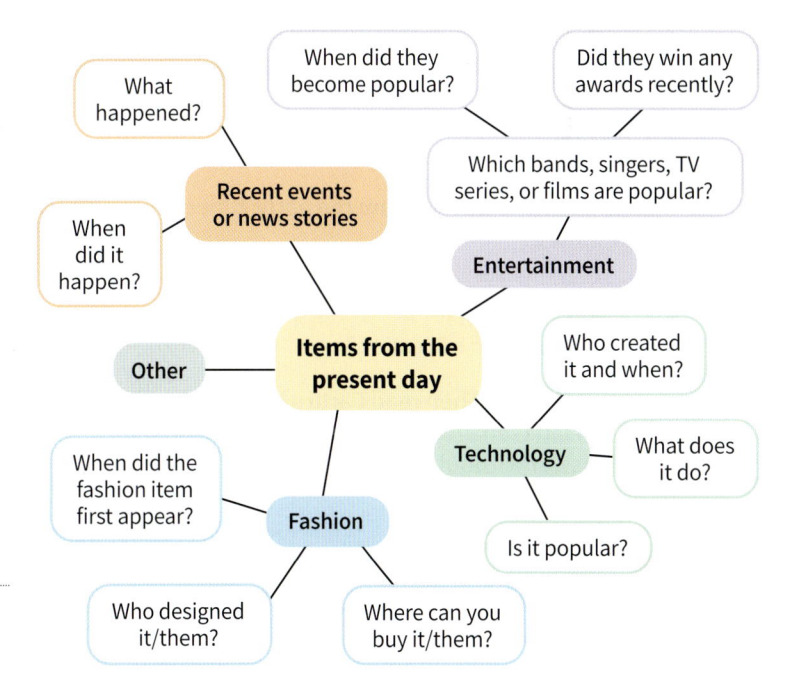

Mind map – **Items from the present day**:
- Recent events or news stories: What happened? When did they become popular? When did it happen?
- Entertainment: Did they win any awards recently? Which bands, singers, TV series, or films are popular?
- Technology: Who created it and when? What does it do? Is it popular?
- Fashion: When did the fashion item first appear? Who designed it/them? Where can you buy it/them?
- Other

13 Discuss ways to present the items in your time capsule.
> I can search for an article about Netflix.

1.3 THE BIRTH OF TEENAGE CULTURE

LESSON OBJECTIVES
- Learn about the beginning of teenage culture in the USA
- Read for overall meaning (gist) • Talk about the past using *was* / *were*

Carla's Blog

About **New posts**

Hi! My name's Carla. I come from California in the USA, and I really love history. You probably know quite a lot about teens like me from American TV shows and movies. But what were American teenagers like in 1900?

Well, first of all, the word *teenager* didn't exist! There weren't any 'teenagers' like us in 1900. You were a child, then you got a job, and then you were an adult! In 1900, children could leave school at 14 to work, and most did. Eighteen per cent of all working Americans were under the age of 16.

Was work better than school? No, it wasn't. Life was very hard for working teens. Many of them worked in coal mines or cotton mills for long hours. The work wasn't well paid, and it was often dangerous. Unfortunately, for most families, there wasn't a choice. They needed the money to pay for basic things like food and clothes.

Luckily, in the 1920s and 30s, things got better. People had more money and there were new laws about education and work. More teenagers went to school, from an average of about 100 days per year in 1900 to 143 days in 1930, and they stayed in education longer. There was time for sports, music, and hanging out! For the first time, teenagers developed their own identity. This was the birth of teenage culture.

READING

1 Look at photos A–C from the early 20th century. Which photo shows:
1 .... teenagers relaxing and having fun?
2 .... a teenager at work?
3 .... teenagers in education?

2 Read the *Skill UP!* Then read Carla's blog for the gist. How did life change for American teenagers between the 1900s and the 1930s? Try to answer without using a dictionary.

> **Skill UP!** When you read a text for the first time, don't stop for words and phrases you don't know. Read the whole text quickly, and focus on the parts you understand. This will help you get the gist, or overall meaning of the text.

3 Give definitions, examples or synonyms for these words from the blog.

adult choice dangerous identity laws modern well paid

4 🔊 01 Read the article again and listen. Are the sentences true (T) or false (F)? Correct the false sentences.
1 Nobody used the word *teenager* in 1900. ....
2 In 1900, 16% of Americans with a job were under the age of 18. ....
3 Working teenagers weren't paid a lot of money in 1900. ....
4 Americans were generally richer in the 1920s and 30s than they were in 1900. ....
5 Teenagers spent less time at school per year in 1930 than they did in 1900. ....

5 **THINK** Why is it better for young teenagers to go to school and not work?

> **LIFE SKILLS** It is important to be aware of your own development during your teenage years. How are you different to a child? How are you different to an adult?

GRAMMAR

Past simple: (*there*) *was / were*; past time phrases

6 Study the highlighted language in Carla's blog. Then complete the table.

	Affirmative	Negative
I / He / She / It	**was**	¹
We / You / They	²	**weren't**
There	**was / were**	**wasn't** / ³
Questions	Short answers	
Was I / he / she / it … ?	Yes, I / he / she / it **was**.	No, I / he / she / it ⁴ .
Were you / we / they … ?	Yes, you / we / they **were**.	No, you / we / they **weren't**.

CHECK IT! ➔ MY GRAMMAR REFERENCE & PRACTICE p106

7 Underline more examples of the past simple form of *be* in Carla's blog.

8 Complete the sentences with the correct form of the verb *be*. Make them true for you.
1 My great grandparents _____ alive in 1900.
2 There _____ time to hang out with my friends before school this morning.
3 My parents _____ born in the same country.
4 I _____ awake at midnight last night.
5 The last film I saw _____ very good.
6 My friends _____ happy last time I saw them.

9 💬 Complete the questions with the correct form of the verb *be*. Then ask and answer with a partner.
1 _____ you tired when you woke up this morning?
2 _____ yesterday a good day? Why / Why not?
3 What _____ your favourite food when you were a young child?
4 Where _____ you born?
5 What _____ the best class at school yesterday?
6 _____ there any students in the classroom when you arrived for your English class today?

✓ We use past time phrases with the past simple to say exactly when things happened.

10 Look at the past time phrases in the box. How many can you find in exercises 8 and 9 above?

in 1900 – exercise 8

an hour ago   on Friday evening
at midnight last night   over the summer holidays
~~in 1900~~   this morning   in the 1920s and 30s
two weeks ago   last week   yesterday

11 Put the past time phrases from exercise 10 in order. Start with the most recent.

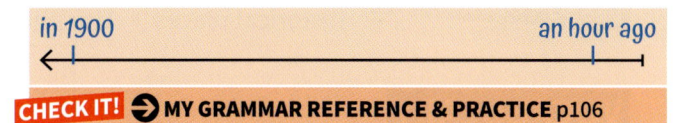

in 1900 ←————————————————→ an hour ago

CHECK IT! ➔ MY GRAMMAR REFERENCE & PRACTICE p106

12 💬 Complete the task. Then change roles.
Student A Ask three questions using three different past time phrases. Then guess Student B's false answer.
Student B Listen to Student A's questions. Give two true answers and one false answer.

> Question 1: Where were you on Friday evening?
>> I was at home.
> Question 2: Where were you over the summer holidays?
>> I was in Jamaica.
> OK, question 3: Where were you an hour ago?
>> I was in a maths class.
> I think your answer to question 2 was false.
>> You're right! Now ask me.

PROJECT BUILDER 3

Complete a personal profile.

➔ Workbook **Project Log** p5

13 Complete the profile about you.
Favourite thing to do over the summer holidays: go to the beach

About me
1 Favourite thing to do over the summer holidays:
2 Favourite thing to do with friends:
3 Favourite sport or outdoor activity:
4 Favourite piece of technology:
5 Favourite game, book or film:
6 Favourite school subjects:

14 Add one more 'favourite' to your personal profile.

15 👥 Imagine it is 2060. Interview each other about the details on your profiles.

> What was your favourite thing to do over the summer holidays when you were a teenager?
>> It was to go to the beach.

1.4 CREEPY PLACES!

LESSON OBJECTIVES • Describe feelings with adjectives • Listen to teenagers talking about creepy historical places • Use photos and labels to predict vocabulary

VOCABULARY

1 Read Lucia and Hugo's online messages. What do you learn about the ship in the photo?

2 **MEDIATION** A friend doesn't understand the word 'creepy'. Write a definition of 'a creepy place' in your own language.

3 Match the emojis in the online messages to six of the adjectives in the box.

annoyed	bored	embarrassed
excited	relaxed	scared
surprised	tired	unhappy
worried		

4 🔊 02 Listen to Lucia and Hugo. What are they feeling? Match 1–4 to four of the adjectives from exercise 3.

5 Work in groups of three or four. Which emojis do you use most often? Which are your favourites?

6 In your group, take turns miming and guessing the feelings in exercise 3. Who guessed the most correctly?

Lucia Hi Hugo. How's your holiday going? It rained all day here. There's nothing to do. I'm so ¹ 🤔.

Hugo Hi Lucia. Fuerteventura is great. Today we tried kitesurfing and saw a shipwreck!

Lucia Woah! Awesome.

Hugo I was so ² 😀 about the kitesurfing, but also a bit ³ 😕. It was great, but really difficult.

Lucia Cool! What about the shipwreck?

Hugo It was so creepy! The ship is more than 80 years old. You can read about it online – it has a very interesting history. In 1994, there was an accident and now it's stuck. Poor Miguel got really ⁴ 😨 and then felt a bit ⁵ 😟. We just got back to the campsite. I'm so ⁶ 😴.

Lucia Poor Miguel! Enjoy the rest of your holiday.

LISTENING

7 In exercise 8, you will hear three teenagers talking about the places in photos A–C. First, read the *Skill UP!* and try to predict the vocabulary you will hear. Write a list.

> **Skill UP!** Before you listen, prepare by looking at pictures and labels. Use them to predict the vocabulary you will hear.

shopping mall, fish, ...

A New World Shopping Mall
Bangkok, Thailand

B Maunsell Sea Forts
Thames Estuary, Great Britain

C Explorer Scott's hut
Cape Evans, Antarctica

8 🔊 03 Listen for the vocabulary from your list in exercise 7. Tick the items you hear.

9 🔊 03 Listen again and complete the sentences.
1 _____ destroyed the roof of the shopping mall.
2 Noi says people are _____ when they see photos of the fish in the mall.
3 Britain built the Maunsell Sea Forts in _____.
4 Tom says the forts were creepy, but he wasn't _____.
5 Julieta's mum is a _____ in Antarctica.
6 In Scott's hut there are still _____, tinned food and equipment.

10 💬 Discuss the questions.
1 Which place in this lesson do you think is the creepiest? Which would you most like to see?
2 Where is the creepiest place you know? Is it somewhere real, or is it from a story, film or TV series?
3 Choose three feelings from the box in exercise 3. Say when you last felt this way, where you were and what happened.

11 💬 **MEDIATION** Look online and take a virtual tour of Scott's hut. Find three interesting things inside and outside the hut. Tell the class in English.

PROJECT BUILDER 4

Write a description of an interesting place that you know.

➡ Workbook **Project Log** p5

12 👥 Think of places you know in your town or city that will be interesting to people in the future. They can be:
- creepy places, e.g. an old building
- new places, e.g. a new shopping centre
- your school

13 Choose one place each to write about for your time capsule. Describe the place:
- Where is it?
- What does it look like?
- Can you give any interesting details about the place, e.g. its history?
- How does the place make you feel, e.g. relaxed, excited, scared?

Near our school, there is a street called West Road. Number 78 is a creepy old house. It looks like a house from a horror film! Once I walked past it at night and I thought I saw a person in the window. I was very scared because I know that nobody lives there. Is the house still there?

14 At home, find photos of your interesting place.

15

1.5 TODAY'S HEROES

LESSON OBJECTIVES
- Talk about your heroes
- Make and respond to suggestions
- Learn how to show interest during conversations

SPEAKING

1 💬 Discuss the questions.
1 Who are your heroes and why?
2 What would you like to say to them?
3 How do heroes change the world?

2 💬 Read the factfiles below.

Young heroes

Amandla Stenberg
About: Amandla appeared in *The Hunger Games* with Jennifer Lawrence.
Born: 1998, California, USA
What makes them a hero: Amandla fights for women's rights and against racism. She's a ¹_____ hero.
Actor

Fionn Ferreira
About: Fionn won the 2019 Google Science Fair.
Born: 2000, Cork, Ireland
What makes them a hero: Fionn found a way to remove ²_____ pollution from water. He's an ³_____ hero.
Scientist and engineer

Simone Biles
About: Simone became the greatest female gymnast ever.
Born: 1997, Ohio, USA
What makes them a hero: Simone won 25 World Gymnastics Championships ⁴_____. She's a ⁵_____ hero.
Gymnast

3 Complete the factfiles with the words in the box.

> environmental   human rights
> sporting   plastic   medals

4 ▶Video Watch the first part of the video. Answer the questions.
1 What is Lucy and Amy's homework?
2 Who do they choose to write about from exercise 2?

5 ▶Video Complete the *Key phrases*. Then watch again and check.

KEY PHRASES
Making and responding to suggestions

Making suggestions

We ¹_____ (choose) …	³_____ don't we (choose) … ?
How ²_____ (choosing) … ?	Maybe (Amandla Stenberg).
Let's (think of …) instead.	

Agreeing with suggestions

That sounds good.	That's a great ⁴_____ !

Disagreeing with suggestions

I'm not so ⁵_____ on that idea.
I'm not ⁶_____ about (that).
I'd rather not (write about) …

6 ▶Video Look at the photo. How do you think Lucy and Amy feel? Can you guess why? Watch the second part of the video and check.

7 🔊 04 Read the *Skill UP!* Then listen and number the phrases for expressing surprise in order from 1–3.

Skill UP! Show interest during conversations by listening carefully, asking the other person questions, responding to their answers and expressing surprise.

> Seriously? ___   No way! ___
> That's incredible! ___

8 💬 Discuss and choose a hero for each category in the box. Use the *Key phrases* during your discussion.

> celebrity heroes   sporting heroes   teenage heroes

1.6 A FUN DAY OUT

LESSON OBJECTIVES • Write a personal message • Use linkers

WRITING

1 💬 Think about your answers to the questions. Then tell a partner.
1 When was the last time you had a fun day out?
2 Where did you go?
3 Who did you go with?
4 What did you do?
5 How did you feel?

2 Read the message that Raya put in her group's time capsule. What did she do on her fun day out?

To the people of the future,

Hi! How are you? I hope you're well. Congratulations on finding our time capsule! I'm writing to tell you about a fun day out in our time.

My last birthday is a good example. First, my friends and I went to the Metro shopping centre. Next, we ate pizza at Ginelli's restaurant. Is pizza still popular in your time?

After that, we went to a virtual reality centre. Do you know what that is? We put on special headsets and played a virtual reality game together. I was really excited, and also a bit nervous. At the end of the day, my friends gave me a cool new phone case for my birthday.

Is a fun day out for teenagers very different in the future?

Best wishes,
Raya

3 Read Raya's message again and put the events in order from 1–4.
A ___ Describe a recent fun day out.
B ___ Explain why you are writing.
C ___ Say hi and ask about the person / people you are writing to.
D ___ Finish your message with a question for the reader and your name.

4 Read the Skill UP! Then complete it with linkers from Raya's message.

Skill UP! Using linkers
Use linkers to describe what happened in the right order.
Beginning: *First of all* / ___
Middle: *Next* / *Later* / ___
End: *Finally* / ___

5 Use linkers and the prompts below to write a short description of a fun day out.

LAST SATURDAY
• Meet my friends at the beach.
• Go swimming in the sea.
• Have some ice cream.
• Go to a burger restaurant.
• Be very tired.

Last Saturday, I had a fun day out. First of all, I met my friends at the beach, ...

PROJECT BUILDER 5

Write a personal message.
➡ Workbook **Project Log** p6

6 Write a personal message about a fun day out to put in your group's time capsule.

A Plan
• Remember or invent a fun day out and make notes using the questions in exercise 1.
• Use the steps in exercise 3 to plan your message.
• Think of one or two questions to ask the people of the future.

B Write
• Use linkers to describe the order of events.
• Write two paragraphs about the fun day out.
• Mention how you felt.

C Read and check
• Check your message includes all the necessary information.
• Check your spelling.

1 PROJECT

Create a time capsule

SHARE AND REVIEW

1 Look back at your Project Builders 1–5 for this unit. In which Project Builder did you:
   - A describe an interesting place that you know?   4
   - B choose items to go in your time capsule?   ......
   - C write a message about a fun day out?   ......
   - D complete a personal profile?   ......
   - E write a note for the people who find your time capsule?   ......

2 Share and review the work from your Project Builders. Is there anything you want to change?

Use your Project Log → p4–6

DECIDE

PROJECT SKILLS Deciding together
- Work as a group when making decisions about your project.
- Make sure everyone in the group speaks during discussions.
- Listen to everyone's ideas and opinions.
- Give honest feedback to others, but show respect.
- Try to agree on a decision that everyone is happy with. If you can't, vote as a group.

PROJECT COACH ▶ Video

3 🔊 05 Read the *Project skills*, then listen to Mia, Claire and Ryan talking about their time capsule. Choose the correct option.
   1 They decide to write the information about their time capsule items and photos:
      A on labels.
      B on the back of the photos.
      C on a contents page.
   2 They decide to make their time capsule from:
      A a metal container.
      B a shoe box.
      C an envelope.

4 Work together and decide on:
   1 how to include the information about the items in your time capsule.
   2 what container to use for your time capsule.
   3 where you will hide your time capsule.

CREATE

5 Create your time capsule.
- Choose one of your notes from Project Builder 1 and put it in the time capsule.
- Write information about your items using your work from Project Builder 2. Put the items and the information in the time capsule.
- Put all the group's work from Project Builders 3, 4 and 5 in the time capsule.
- Remember to write the year when you want people to open the time capsule on the outside of the container, e.g. *Open in the year 2040*.

PRESENT

6 Present some of the items in your time capsule to the class. Give reasons for your choices. Use the *Key phrases* to help you.

KEY PHRASES
Giving reasons
- We put this in our time capsule because …
- We chose this because …
- This shows that … is / are important in the present day.

7 Walk around the class and look at other groups' time capsules. What are your favourite things?

REFLECT

8 Think about your project work in this unit. Read the statements and choose your reaction.

COLLABORATION
1 Our group can make good decisions together.

CREATIVITY
2 Our group can make an interesting time capsule.

COMMUNICATION
3 Our group can listen to each other's ideas carefully and with respect.

9 Complete these sentences for you.
1 I am pleased with our time capsule because
2 I want to improve

➔ Workbook **Project Log** p7

2 Art and design

UNIT OBJECTIVES

YOUR PROJECT Create an art and design gallery

Project Builders 1–5:
1. Plan your art and design gallery.
2. Design and describe your own piece of street art.
3. Create a group portrait.
4. Plan a design exhibit.
5. Create an illustrated story.

Display your art and design gallery.

VOCABULARY
- Adjectives and synonyms
- Materials

GRAMMAR
- Past continuous
- Past continuous and past simple; connecting past actions with *as*

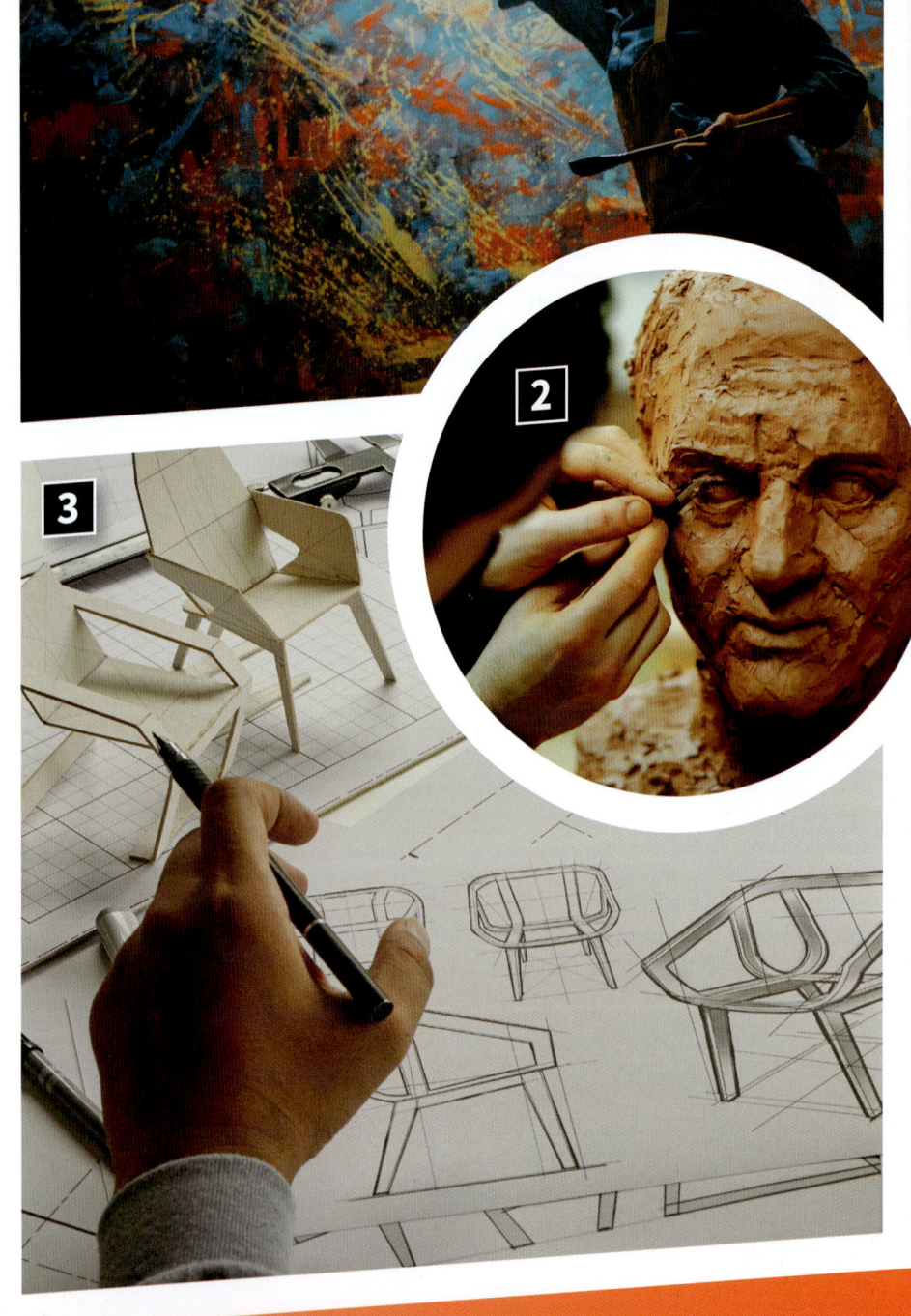

LESSON OBJECTIVES • Learn art vocabulary • Talk about art

WARM-UP

1 Look at photos 1–4. What types of art can you see? _____

2 💬 Complete the table. Then discuss your favourite types of art.

Art	dance	design	³ _____	music	⁵ _____	⁶ _____	sculpture	street art
Artist	¹ _____	² _____	illustrator	⁴ _____	painter	photographer	⁷ _____	street ⁸ _____

3 💬 Which three types of artist do you admire the most? Why?

> I admire dancers. They use their bodies to make art. They are very strong and their movements are beautiful.

4 ▶Video Watch Curtis and Amanda's vlog. Why do they go to an art gallery?

5 ▶Video Are the sentences true (T) or false (F)? Watch again and check.
1 Amanda has 15 minutes to paint Curtis's portrait. _____
2 Curtis thinks Amanda's paintings look like him. _____
3 Curtis and Amanda enjoyed their visit to the art gallery. _____
4 Curtis doesn't think Amanda is a good sculptor. _____
5 There was a street art exhibit at the art gallery. _____
6 Curtis paints a perfect portrait of Amanda. _____

Curtis and Amanda's VLOG
Today we're doing art

6 💬 Discuss the questions.
1 Do you enjoy making art? Which types?
2 Can you think of an example of a piece of art or a famous artist that you like?

PROJECT BUILDER 1 Plan your art and design gallery.

➔ Workbook **Project Log** p8

7 Design and draw a plan of your gallery. Include the following rooms and features.

Exhibition rooms

Street art	Design
Paintings	Illustrations

Features

- 🚪 Entrance
- 🧥 Cloakroom
- 🚻 Toilets
- 🎁 Gift shop
- ☕ Café

8 Which direction will visitors take through your gallery? Add arrows (→) to your plan.

9 Think of a name for your gallery.

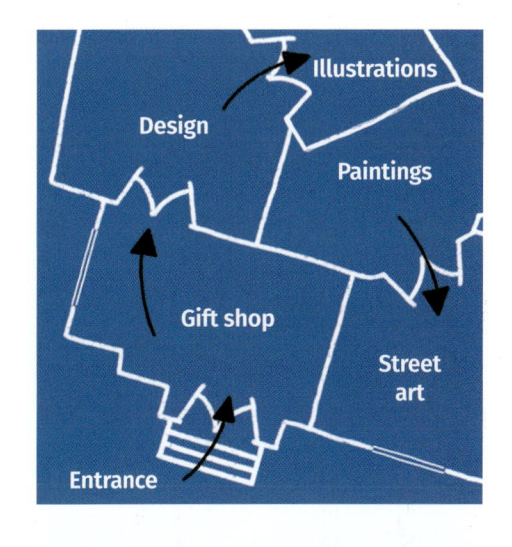

2.2 STREET ART

LESSON OBJECTIVES
- Learn about different types of street art
- Learn adjectives and their synonyms
- Use the past continuous to talk about actions in progress in the past

1 Look at photos A–E on the web page. Which is your favourite? Why?

2 Match descriptions 1–5 to the examples of street art A–E. Use the comments on the web page to help you.
1 .... It's very large.
2 .... It took a whole day to make.
3 .... It's good for selfies.
4 .... It makes people laugh.
5 .... It's made with stones.

VOCABULARY

3 Match the adjectives in the box to the highlighted synonyms in the web page.

| attractive | ~~bright~~ | brilliant |
| enormous | terrible | unusual |

bright – colourful
....
....
....
....

4 💬 Are there any differences in meaning between the synonyms? Discuss.

> My pink trainers are bright but they're not colourful. They're just one colour.

> You're right. Rainbows are colourful because they have lots of different colours. They're bright *and* colourful.

Look UP! Look online and find one more example of each type of street art from the web page. Which adjectives from this lesson describe your examples?

5 💬 **MEDIATION** Imagine you are talking to an older adult who doesn't speak English. Tell them about three types of street art in your own language.

Our **S**pectacular **S**treets | Street artists | Your favourites | Your photos

The streets are our gallery

A

👤 **BluJude102:**
A local artist did this incredible 3D drawing. She was working on it all day.

OSS: Brilliant photo! 3D street art like this takes a long time and a lot of patience. Were you watching for a long time?

BlueJude102: No, we weren't. My mum and I watched her for about ten minutes in the morning, but then we saw her again in the evening and she was still working!

👤 **Q-becca22:**
This unusual urban mural is in Lyon, where I live. Look carefully! The whole thing is a huge painting.

OSS: It's enormous! This mural really makes the buildings look more attractive.

B

C

👤 **PrinceT_HK:**
I saw this in Australia. People were really enjoying it. They were taking selfies. What's this colourful kind of street art called?

OSS: So pretty! It's called urban knitting or yarn bombing. The bright colours look great in photos!

👤 **worldgirl#9:**
My friend and I were jogging on the beach the other day. We saw these strange balance sculptures. We tried to make one, but it was terrible! I wasn't concentrating and I knocked it over!

OSS: Don't worry. It's very difficult. We tried to make one and ours was awful, too!

D

E

👤 **Bassface99:**
I saw this funny public sculpture in Brussels, in Belgium. People were smiling and laughing and taking photos.

OSS: That's brilliant! This sculpture is called the *Vaartkapoen*. We love art that makes people happy 😀

GRAMMAR
Past continuous

6 Find examples of past continuous forms in the web page comments on page 22.

She was working on it all day.

7 Complete the table using language from the web page.

Affirmative	Verb + -ing
I / He / She / It was	
We / You / They ¹ _____	working on it all day.
Negative	³ _____ selfies.
I / He / She / It ² _____	enjoying it. concentrating.
We / You / They weren't	
Questions	Short answers
Was I / he / she / it ⁴ _____ on it all day?	Yes, I / he / she / it was. No, I / he / she / it wasn't.
⁵ _____ we / you / they watching for a long time?	Yes, we / you / they were. No, we / you / they ⁶ _____.

We use the **past continuous** for ⁷ **actions in progress** / **finished actions** in the past.

CHECK IT! ➡ MY GRAMMAR REFERENCE & PRACTICE p108

8 Complete each sentence with a verb from the box in the correct form.

> paint   shine   sit   take   watch   work

1 An artist was _____ a mural in the town centre yesterday.
2 Lots of people were _____ her paint.
3 Some people were _____ photos of her.
4 She was _____ for a long time.
5 We were _____ there for about 30 minutes.
6 It was relaxing. The sky was clear and the sun was _____.

9 Write sentences using the past continuous.
1 Yesterday afternoon / I / be / swim / the sea.
2 What / be / you / watch / at 9 p.m. last night?
3 I / be not / listen / and I missed the instructions.
4 She / be not / tell / the truth.
5 A Be / you / talk / to me?   B No / I / be not.
6 A Be / they / wait / for you?   B Yes / they / be.

10 Complete the comments with the past continuous form of the verbs in brackets.

Reverse graffiti

Millie08:
I ¹ _____ (feel) bored on Saturday so I went for a walk. Two people ² _____ (clean) a wall at the end of our street … well that's what I thought. Then I saw this – they ³ _____ (draw) a picture!

OSS: Nice photo! ⁴ _____ (you look for) street art? Because, you found it! You were right. The people ⁵ _____ (not clean) the wall. They ⁶ _____ (do) street art. This is called reverse graffiti!

11 💬 Ask and answer about things you were doing yesterday at the times in the box. Were you ever both doing the same thing at the same time?

> 7 a.m.   12 p.m.   6.30 p.m.   10.30 p.m.   12 a.m.

- What were you doing at 10.30 p.m. yesterday?
- I was watching TV. What were you doing?
- I wasn't watching TV, I was playing a video game. What were you doing at … ?

PROJECT BUILDER 2

Design and describe your own piece of street art.

➡ Workbook **Project Log** p8

12 👥 Agree on which types of street art to include in your gallery. Each choose a different type.

13 Imagine you are street artists. Draw your own design to put in your gallery.

14 Write a short paragraph to go in your gallery with your design. Use adjectives from this lesson.

The artist was working on a project at school. She was thinking about the important things in her life. She made this unusual and attractive piece of balance sculpture. It's made from a backpack, a skateboard, photos, a games console and a phone. It's called 'My balance'.

2.3 YOU KNOW THE PICTURE, BUT DID YOU KNOW … ?

LESSON OBJECTIVES
- Learn about famous works of art
- Focus on the most important words when reading
- Use the past continuous and past simple to talk about the past

READING

1 💬 What do you know about the two paintings in the text?

2 Read the *Skill UP!* Then study the words in the boxes. Are they nouns (N), verbs (V) or adjectives (ADJ)? Some can be more than one type.

Skill UP! When you read a text in English, focus on nouns, main verbs and adjectives. These words tell you the most important information.

How *Mona Lisa* became so famous
caught   coat   crime   famous   hid   museum
Paris   police   reported   returned   stole

How Edvard Munch got the idea for *The Scream*
blood red   frightened   heard   ill   painted
scary   scream   sky   sunset   tired   walk

3 🔊 06 Use the words in exercise 2 to predict what the article might say about *Mona Lisa* and *The Scream*. Then read and listen. Check your predictions.

4 Complete the summaries with words from exercise 2.

How *Mona Lisa* became so famous
1 Vincenzo Peruggia ¹_____ *Mona Lisa* from a ²_____. He ³_____ the painting under his ⁴_____ and walked out. Newspapers ⁵_____ the crime around the world. Two years later, ⁶_____ caught Peruggia. They ⁷_____ *Mona Lisa* to Paris.

How Edvard Munch got the idea for *The Scream*
2 At sunset, Edvard Munch was taking a ⁸_____ with friends. The ⁹_____ was ¹⁰_____. Munch was tired and ¹¹_____ at the time. He suddenly felt very ¹²_____. He imagined he ¹³_____ a loud scream. Later, he ¹⁴_____ his experience.

5 💬 **MEDIATION** Imagine you are talking to an English-speaking friend about the article. Choose one of the paintings and say what you learned about it.

Look UP! Look online and find funny recreations of *Mona Lisa* and *The Scream*. Which is the funniest?

You know the paintings and the painters. Now read the interesting stories about some of the world's greatest works of art.

Mona Lisa

We all know *Mona Lisa*'s mysterious smile, but not many people know how she became world famous. In 1911, a man called Vincenzo Peruggia stole Leonardo da Vinci's painting from the Louvre Museum, in Paris. Peruggia was working at the museum when he stole *Mona Lisa*. His plan was simple, but it worked perfectly. He entered the museum early one morning, and waited until nobody was watching. Then he removed the frame from *Mona Lisa*, hid the painting under his coat, and walked out. Newspapers reported the crime and suddenly the whole world was talking about *Mona Lisa*. Two years later, police caught Peruggia and the famous painting was returned to the Louvre.

Did you know? *Mona Lisa* receives so many love letters, she has her own mail box at the Louvre Museum, in Paris!

Edvard Munch painted *The Scream*. He explained in his diary how he got the idea for it. One evening, as the sun was setting, Munch was walking with two friends. During the walk, the sky became blood red and the Norwegian artist suddenly felt very frightened. He was tired and ill at the time, and he imagined he heard a loud and scary scream. Later, he painted his experience. *The Scream* became one of the most famous and expensive paintings in the history of art.

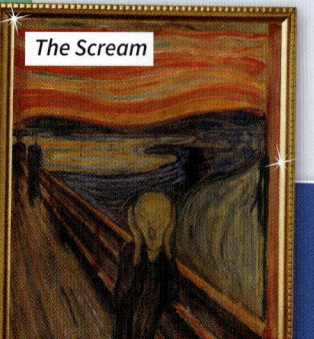

The Scream

Did you know? Munch painted four versions of *The Scream*. Three are in museums and, in 2012, the fourth sold for $119.9 million!

GRAMMAR

Past continuous and past simple

6 Read the underlined sentence in the article. Then match sentences A and B with points 1 and 2 on the timeline.
   A Peruggia stole *Mona Lisa*.
   B Peruggia was working at the museum.

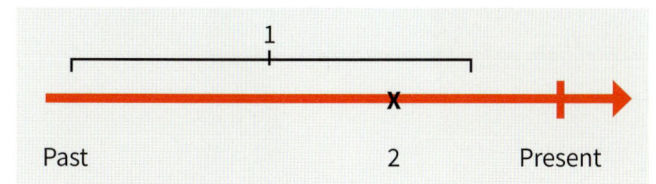

```
          1
    |----------|
————————x—————|——————>
Past        2        Present
```

7 Complete the table.

Past continuous		Past simple	
I / He / She / It **was**	**working** at the museum	when I / he / she / it / we / you / they **stole** *Mona Lisa*.	
We / You / They ¹_____			
Questions			
² _____ he	**working** at the museum	when he	**stole** *Mona Lisa*?
³ _____ you		when you	
Past simple		**Past continuous**	
I / He / She / It / We / You / They	**stole** *Mona Lisa*	while I / he / she / it **was working**	at the museum.
		while we / you / they **were working**	
Questions			
⁴ _____ he	**steal** *Mona Lisa*	while he **was working**	at the museum?
Did you		while you **were working**	

We often use ⁵ **when** / **while** before the past simple and ⁶ **when** / **while** before the past continuous.

CHECK IT! → MY GRAMMAR REFERENCE & PRACTICE p108

8 Complete the sentences with the correct past simple or past continuous form of the verbs in brackets. Use the verbs in the correct order.
   1 My parents _____ while they _____. (meet / study)
   2 My friend _____ me while I _____ my homework (do / call).
   3 When I _____ at school, my friends _____ for me. (arrive / wait)
   4 It _____ when I _____ to bed last night. (go / rain)

9 Write questions for the sentences in exercise 8. Change pronouns when necessary.
   Were you sleeping when your alarm went off?

10 💬 Ask and answer your questions from exercise 9.

11 Read the sentence, then complete the rule.
   As the sun was setting, Munch was walking with two friends.

> We use *as* to connect two actions in the ¹ **past simple** / **past continuous**, to show that the actions were in progress at ² **the same time** / **different times**.

12 💬 Take turns making sentences using *as* and the words in the box. Do your partner's sentences make sense?

> brush teeth   do homework   have a shower
> have breakfast   listen to music   sing   watch TV

As I was having a shower this morning, I was doing my homework.

That doesn't make sense! You can't do homework in the shower!

PROJECT BUILDER 3

Create a group portrait.

→ Workbook **Project Log** p9

13 Read the rules of the challenge.
   1 Your challenge is to take a group photo, then make it look like a portrait painting.
   2 The image must show an emotion, e.g. fear or happiness.
   3 Each person in the image must be in a different position, e.g. sitting, standing, jumping.
   4 You must all have a digital copy of the photo to work with at home.

14 Share your ideas, choose an emotion, then take the photo.

15 Write a short description of your group portrait to put in your gallery.
   We were trying to show the emotion 'excitement' when we created our group portrait. When we took the photo, Liam was sitting on a chair with his hands in the air, Rosa was jumping, and Anthony was standing close to the camera with an excited face. We are very happy with our portrait!

16 Use apps, filters or websites to add effects to your photo and make it look like a painting. Try searching online for 'turn a photo into a painting for free'. Share a copy of the finished image with everyone in your group.

25

2.4 LOOKS GOOD, WORKS WELL

LESSON OBJECTIVES • Learn materials vocabulary • Listen for context • Learn about design

VOCABULARY

1 What are items A–I made of? Match them with the materials in the box.

| cardboard | cotton | glass | leather | metal |
| paper | plastic | wood | wool | |

2 💬 Say what each object A–I is made of.

> The phone case is made of wood.

3 💬 Which are your favourite three things from the photos?

> I like the paper unicorn, the wood phone case and …

4 👥 Work as a group. Search the classroom and look for one item made of each material. You have two minutes. Then tell the class what you found. Which group found the most materials?

> We found a pencil made of wood, a scarf made of wool, a …

A phone case

B chair

C perfume bottle

D unicorn

E boots

F sunglasses

G water bottle

H hat

I T-shirt

LISTENING

5 🔊 07 Read the *Skill UP!* Then listen to the first part of a podcast and answer the three questions.

> **Skill UP!** At the beginning of a podcast there is usually important information about context. Listen and ask yourself three questions:
> Who are the speakers?
> Where are they?
> What are they talking about?
> The answers will help you understand the rest of the podcast.

6 💬 What do you think Marlena and Zara might talk about in the interview?

7 🔊 08 Listen to the next part of the podcast. Which two items A–I from exercise 1 does Zara mention?

8 🔊 08 Listen again. Which two pieces of advice does Zara give to young people interested in design?

9 🔊 09 Complete the sentences with words from the podcast. Then listen and check.
1. As I was travelling to school, I was _____.
2. Well-designed things look good, _____ well, _____ nice, and are eco-friendly.
3. Light, strong, cheap and surprisingly _____.
4. There are websites where you can design your own products, like clothes and _____, for example.

> **LIFE SKILLS** Be a good listener. Make eye contact and nod your head. Use noises like 'mm' and 'uh-huh', and words and phrases like 'right', 'OK' and 'really?' to show you are listening. Why is it important to be a good listener?

10 **THINK** Discuss the questions with a partner. Use the *Key phrases* to help you.
1. What do you own that is well designed? What do you like about it/them?
2. What do you own that is badly designed? What's wrong with it/them?

> **KEY PHRASES**
> **Talking about design**
> … is nice / not nice to look at.   … is easy / difficult to use.
> … works well / doesn't work properly.   … is good / poor quality.
> … feels / doesn't feel nice.   … is / isn't eco-friendly.

11 **MEDIATION** Look online and find a website in English where you can design your own trainers. Tell the class three things about how to design your own trainers in your own language.

PROJECT BUILDER 4 Plan a design exhibit.

→ Workbook **Project Log** p9

12 What types of products are you interested in? Choose one type from the box or think of your own idea.

> backpacks / bags   cars   clothing   computers
> electronic gadgets   jewellery   posters
> shoes / trainers   sports equipment

13 👥 Tell your group about the type of product you chose and your favourite brand or model.
- What do you like about it?
- What is it made of?
- What else do you know about it?

> I love cars and I think Porsches are really well designed. They are great quality, nice to look at and very, very fast! They are made of many different materials like metal, glass and plastic. Unfortunately, they aren't very eco-friendly.

14 Plan your design exhibit for your gallery.
- What will your exhibit be called?
  Porsche: Speed and Beauty
- What information about your brand or model do you want to include in your exhibit? Write three to five questions.
  - *When did Porsche start?*
  - *Who started it?*
  - *What was Porsche's first car called?*
  - *What materials did they use in their first car?*
- What pictures do you need to find?
  An old Porsche, a new Porsche, a picture of Ferdinand Porsche (the man who started the company) …

15 Find the information and pictures you need.

27

2.5 TELL ME WHAT YOU SEE

LESSON OBJECTIVES • Describe a scene • Explain unknown words

A Breakdancing
B Free-style football

SPEAKING

1 💬 Look at photos A and B of street performers and discuss the questions.
   1 Who are the people and where are they?
   2 What are they doing in the photo?

2 ▶Video Watch the first part of the video. Answer the questions.
   1 Why does Marcel call his friend, Caleb?
   2 How does Marcel help Caleb?
   3 Which photo, A or B, is similar to Marcel's video call?

3 ▶Video Watch again. Tick the *Key phrases* the characters use.

KEY PHRASES

Describing a photo or scene

Saying what you can see

I can see …
There is / are …
This is (a photo) of …
This (photo) shows …

Saying where things are

In the (foreground / middle / background), there's …
It's (in front of / behind / near / on top of / under) …
On the (left / right), there's …
The person on the (left / right) is …
Next to (that), there's …

Saying what is happening

He is / They are *-ing* …

4 ▶Video Look at the photo. Can you guess who Marcel saw on his phone? Watch the second part of the video and check.

5 💬 **MEDIATION** Imagine you are talking to an English-speaking friend on your phone. You see the scenes in photos A and B above. With your partner, describe them to your friend using the *Key phrases*.

6 Read the *Skill UP!* Then complete Marcel's description with the words in the box.

Skill UP! When you don't know what something is called in English, try to explain it in your own words. Is it like something else? Can you say what it's made of? Can you describe where and how people use it?

| clean | have | like | made |

In the middle, on the ground, there's a big square of that material … what's it called? It's ¹ .... carpet, but ² .... of plastic. People ³ .... it on their kitchen or bathroom floor because it's easy to ⁴ ....

7 Draw a picture using five of the images below. Put the items in different places on the page, including in the foreground and background. Don't show anyone.

8 💬 Complete the task. Then change roles. Use the *Key phrases* to help you.

Student A Describe your picture to Student B. Don't show your picture to Student B until they finish their drawing.

Student B Listen to Student A and draw their picture.

2.6 WORDS AND PICTURES

LESSON OBJECTIVES • Write and illustrate a story • Make your illustrated story fun to read

WRITING

1 Look at sections 1–4 of the illustrated story. How does Alex help his grandparents to make a lot of money?

[Panel 1] I have an idea! I'll show you the secret room in the roof.
[Panel 2] Woah! Cool!
[Panel 3] This is a copy. The original is worth a lot of money, but nobody knows where it is …
[Panel 4] Calm down Alex!
Two weeks later …
The Daily Echo — Local Couple Sell Missing Painting

2 Now match captions A–D with sections 1–4.

A ___ I was so excited, I ran down the stairs, and tried to explain to my parents. Dad called Grandad, Grandad took the painting to a gallery, and two weeks later my grandparents were rich!

B ___ We climbed the stairs up into the cold, dark roof of the house. Grandad switched on the light. The room was full of strange old things. There were creepy statues, enormous fossils, unusual musical instruments and some colourful paintings. One painting was incredible. Grandad couldn't remember where he got it.

C ___ My name is Alex. Last winter, my sister and I were staying at my grandparents' house. The weather was awful and we were bored, until Grandad had an idea.

D ___ A few weeks later, I was watching a vlog online when suddenly, I saw the incredible painting from Grandad's secret room.

3 Read the story again. In which caption does the writer:
1 **C** say where and when the story is happening?
2 ___ introduce the main character(s)?
3 ___ describe an interesting place?
4 ___ introduce an interesting piece of art?
5 ___ include a dramatic surprise or 'twist'?
6 ___ finish the story with a happy ending?

4 Read the *Skill UP!* Then find examples for points 1–5 in the pictures and captions from exercises 1 and 2.

> **Skill UP!**
> **Making your illustrated story fun to read**
> 1 Use adjectives to describe places and things, e.g. *huge*, *colourful*.
> 2 Use adjectives to describe how characters feel, e.g. *scared*, *happy*.
> 3 Use speech bubbles to show what the characters say, e.g. Woah! Cool!
> 4 Use the word *suddenly* to introduce a dramatic event.
> 5 Use exclamation marks (!) after dramatic events or words.

PROJECT BUILDER 5

Create an illustrated story.

→ Workbook *Project Log* p10

5 Write and illustrate a short story. Include an artist or a piece of art in your story. Work in groups for Part A only.

A Plan
• Choose one of these themes or think of your own.
  1 A teenager becomes a world-famous street artist.
  2 A group of teenagers help police catch an art thief.
  3 A teenager finds a famous missing piece of art.
• Choose one or two main characters.
• Choose an interesting setting for your story.
• Choose a piece of art or an artist to feature in your story.
• Plan four main sections to your story.

B Write and illustrate
• Follow the tips from the *Skill UP!* and write your story.
• Illustrate your story with four pictures.

C Read and check
• Is your story fun to read?
• Check your use of the past continuous.
• Check your spelling and grammar.

29

2 PROJECT

Create an art and design gallery

Use your Project Log → p8–10

SHARE AND REVIEW

1. Look back at your Project Builders 1–5 for this unit. In which Project Builder did you:
   - A write and illustrate a story with an art theme? 5
   - B design and describe a piece of street art? ___
   - C prepare information and pictures for a design exhibit? ___
   - D design your gallery? ___
   - E create and describe a group portrait? ___

2. Share and review the work from your Project Builders. Is there anything you want to change?

DECIDE

3. 🔊 10 Listen to Mia, Ryan, Claire and Sanjay describing different ways to display their project work. Match pictures A–D with students 1–4.

   A ___   B ___

   C ___   D ___

4. Decide on the best way to display your project work.

PROJECT SKILLS Planning and creating your display together
- Plan your time based on how much of it you have to create your display.
- Think about the equipment you need and find it.
- Share the work of creating the display equally between the group members, e.g. work on one exhibition room each.
- If you finish your work early, help the others in your group.

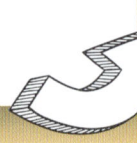

PROJECT COACH ▶ Video

30

CREATE

5 Create your art and design gallery display.
- Follow the advice in the *Project skills*.
- Gather all the group's work from Project Builders 1–5.
- Create your display. Use your gallery plan from Project Builder 1 to help you organize your project work.

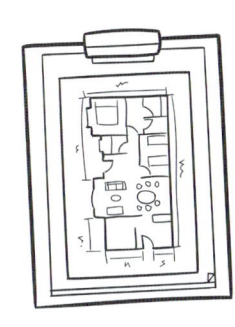

PRESENT

6 Prepare a guided tour for one or more of your gallery's exhibition rooms. Then present it as a group.

> Welcome to a guided tour of our art gallery. On your left is the street art room. The first piece of street art is a balance sculpture called 'My balance' by a street artist called Abby. Abby was working on a project at school. She was thinking about the important things in her life when she made this unusual and attractive sculpture.

7 Walk around the class and look at all the gallery displays. Choose three favourite things from the other groups' projects.

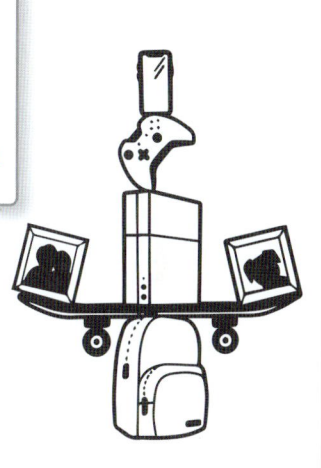

REFLECT

8 Think about your project work in this unit. Read the statements and choose your reaction.

COLLABORATION
1 Members of our group can help each other with project tasks.

CREATIVITY
2 Our group can display project work in different ways.

COMMUNICATION
3 Our group can present clearly.

9 Complete these sentences for you.
1 I am pleased with our art and design gallery because _____
2 I want to improve _____

→ Workbook **Project Log** p11

31

3 Fresh air

UNIT OBJECTIVES

YOUR PROJECT Design a park for the whole community

Project Builders 1–5:
1. Create a simple plan for your park.
2. Choose outdoor activities for different members of the community.
3. Decide which green projects to include.
4. Create a programme of events for your park's opening weekend.
5. Write a speech to give at the opening of your park.

Give your speech and display your park design.

VOCABULARY
- Outdoor activities
- Outdoor events

GRAMMAR
- *will* / *won't* for predictions
- First conditional

LESSON OBJECTIVES • Learn park features • Talk about how different groups of people use parks

WARM-UP

1 💬 Look at the picture of a park. Answer the questions.
   1 What can you see in the park?
   2 What are the people doing?

2 Match the park features in the box with 1–11 in the picture.

| bench   bridge   café   duck pond   lake   open-air theatre |
| outdoor gym   path   picnic area   playground   skatepark |

3 💬 Think of a park that you both know and discuss the questions.
   1 Which features from exercise 2 does the park have?
   2 What do these different groups of people do at the park?
   • families with young children
   • teenagers
   • adults
   • older adults (aged 65+)

   > Teenagers spend time with friends in the park. They also skateboard and …

Curtis and Amanda's VLOG
Designing a park

4 ▶Video Watch Curtis and Amanda's vlog. They are designing a park. Answer the questions.
   1 Which age groups in the community are sharing ideas for the park?
   2 Why doesn't Sarah like Curtis and Amanda's park design?

5 ▶Video Watch again. Complete the table. Match the park features from exercise 2 to the correct zones of Curtis and Amanda's finished park design.

| Family Zone: café, | Action Zone: |
| Quiet Zone: | Eco Zone: |

PROJECT BUILDER 1   Create a simple plan for your park.

↪ Workbook **Project Log** p12

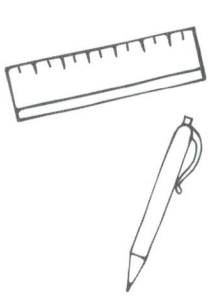

6 👥 Start planning your park by completing a table like the one in exercise 5. Include the four zones and add at least four park features to each zone. Use the features from exercise 2 and your own ideas. You can use the same feature in more than one zone, e.g. benches and paths.

   > Let's have an outdoor gym in the Action Zone. What else?   > What about a … ?

33

3.2 OUTDOOR LIFE

LESSON OBJECTIVES • Learn outdoor activities vocabulary • Use *will* / *won't* for predictions

VOCABULARY

1 🔊 **11** Listen to Amelia, Oliver and Nick talking about outdoor leisure activities. Match the speakers to photos 1–3.

1 .... 2 .... 3 ....

1 Blobbing

2 Bubble football

3 E-mountain biking

2 💬 Would you like to try the activities in the photos? Why / Why not?

> I'd like to try bubble football because it sounds really fun. I'm not sure about blobbing. It sounds a bit scary.

3 Match the outdoor activities in the box to pictures A–J.

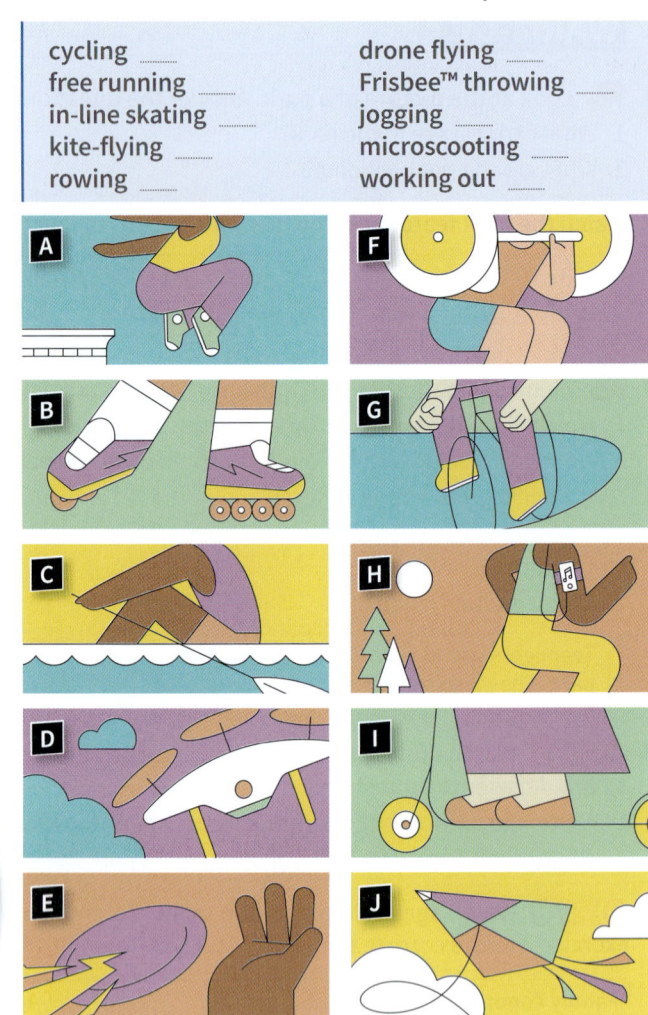

cycling	drone flying ....
free running	Frisbee™ throwing ....
in-line skating	jogging ....
kite-flying	microscooting ....
rowing	working out ....

A B C D E F G H I J

4 💬 Find out what your partner thinks about the activities in exercise 3.

> What do you think about free running?

> I think it's (exciting / brilliant / unusual).

LIFE SKILLS Public spaces, such as parks and playgrounds, are shared by everyone in a community. Everyone who uses them should treat them with respect. What kinds of things should people not do in public spaces?

5 **MEDIATION** Choose three of the outdoor activities from exercise 3, then look online and find videos in English about them. What equipment do you need for them? Are there competitions for these activities? Did you learn any new words during your research? Tell the class in English.

34

6 Read the forum. What features and events does Sydney Park have?

Sydney Life Forum

Meilin I live in Harbin, China. Next month my family and I are moving to St Peters, in Sydney. Is there a park? Will we be able to walk our dogs and go for a run there?

Tom15 Hi. Yes, you will! Sydney Park is in St Peters and it's brilliant! There's lots of space for your dogs to run around. They'll love it!

Meilin Hi and thanks. That sounds great.

Tom15 The park is also really good for keeping fit. There are outdoor gyms and cycling paths. You'll see lots of people running, in-line skating and cycling. There's also a 5 km fun run every Saturday morning.

Meilin I'll definitely do the fun run! What about relaxing?

Tom15 There's lots of wildlife, and some beautiful ponds and picnic areas. There's also a café. For children, there's a really good playground and even a bike track.

Meilin My brother will be happy about the playground!

Tom15 There are even concerts and cultural events.

Meilin It sounds perfect. Thanks for your help!

Tom15 You're welcome. I hope you'll be happy in St Peters. You won't be disappointed by Sydney Park!

GRAMMAR
will / won't for predictions

7 Find examples of *will* and *won't* in the forum. Then complete the table.

Affirmative and negative			
+	I / He / She / It / We / You / They	¹ .... / 'll	definitely do the fun run.
–		won't	
Questions and short answers			
² .... we be able to walk our dogs and go for a run there?			Yes, you **will**.
			No, you ³ ....

We use *will* ('ll) / *won't* + infinitive without *to* to talk about the ⁴ **past** / **future**.

We use the short form *'ll* in ⁵ **formal** / **informal** spoken and written communication.

CHECK IT! ➡ MY GRAMMAR REFERENCE & PRACTICE p110

8 Write predictions using *will* ('ll) or *won't* and the verbs in brackets.
1 Meilin's dogs .... (enjoy) running around in Sydney Park.
2 Meilin likes jogging. She definitely .... (do) the Saturday fun run in Sydney Park.
3 Meilin's little brother can't ride a bike. He .... (not use) the bike track in the park.
4 With Sydney Park so close, Meilin .... (not be) bored.
5 .... Meilin and her family .... (be) happy in St Peters? Yes, they probably ....

9 Complete the predictions so they are true for you. Use *will* ('ll) or *won't* and the verbs in the box. Then compare with a partner.

meet   speak   study   visit

1 I .... another country in the future.
2 I .... at university.
3 My friends and I .... in the park one day next summer.
4 I .... good English when I'm older.

10 💬 Write three predictions about what your partner *will* or *won't* do after school today. Then check with your partner.

> Javier will go microscooting after school.

> Will you go microscooting after school today, Javier?

> Yes, I will.

> I was right!

PROJECT BUILDER 2

Choose outdoor activities for different members of the community.

➡ Workbook **Project Log** p12

11 👥 Look at the park plan you made in Project Builder 1. Predict which outdoor activities from this lesson people will do in your park.

> People will do rowing on our lake.

12 👥 Where will people do the outdoor activities? Match them to the zones in your plan from Project Builder 1.

13 👥 Which of your activities will these different groups of users do?
1 families with young children
2 teenagers
3 adults
4 older adults

> Older adults won't do free running, but they'll go jogging or cycling in our park.

35

3.3 GREENING OUR CITIES

LESSON OBJECTIVES
- Learn about the benefits of urban green spaces
- Use your own knowledge to help you understand a text
- Use the first conditional

Teens for greener cities (TGC)

Plants against pollution
Urban life is attractive, and the world's cities are growing quickly. The United Nations predicts that 68% of humans will live in urban areas by 2050. If more people move into cities, what will happen? Unfortunately, they will get hotter and more polluted, but we can change that. Trees and plants reduce air pollution and keep cities cool. Medellín, in Colombia, is a great example of a city that introduced new plants and trees and became cooler and cleaner as a result.

TGC says ... If we plant more trees in our cities, the air quality will improve.

Medellín, Colombia

A pocket park in New Rochelle, USA

Pocket parks
Most cities and suburbs have a lot of unused pieces of land. These often look bad and make people feel unsafe. Some cities are turning these empty spaces into small parks, called pocket parks. Research shows that pocket parks can reduce crime and stress in a community and increase the amount of exercise people do.

TGC says ... If communities have pocket parks, people will feel safer and healthier.

Nature as our neighbour
Cities are noisy places full of traffic and concrete. This can make them very unattractive to wildlife. All animals need fresh water, birds and bats need trees, and bees and butterflies need wildflowers. If we provide these things in cities, they will be full of life. If our cities are full of plants and wildlife, will they be better places for humans as well? Yes, this will make them nicer and healthier places to live, work and visit. A great example of this is The High Line, in New York.

TGC says ... Cities won't attract wildlife if they don't provide water, trees and wildflowers.

The High Line, New York, USA

READING

1 💬 **MEDIATION** Think of a city you know well. Describe it to your partner in English using the words in the box. Then change roles.

| clean   green spaces   noisy   polluted   quiet   wildlife |

> There are some green spaces, but there isn't a lot of wildlife.

2 💬 Read the *Skill UP!* Then discuss the questions.

> **Skill UP!** Before you read a text, think about what you already know about the topic. As you read, look for those things in the text. This can help you to understand the text and work out the meaning of unknown words.

1 What do you already know about the topic of the leaflet above?
2 How do you think the following things can make urban life better?
- trees and plants
- green spaces and parks
- birds, insects and other wildlife

3 🔊 12 Read and listen to the leaflet. Does it mention any of the things you talked about in exercise 2?

> ✓ A collocation is two or more words that often go together, e.g. *blonde hair, go for a run, hard work*.

4 Complete the collocations with the most suitable verbs from the box. Use examples from the leaflet to help.

| attract   plant   reduce |

1 .... trees / wildflowers / vegetables
2 .... wildlife / birds / insects
3 .... air pollution / crime / stress

36

5 Read the leaflet again. Answer the questions.
 1 How can we reduce heat and air pollution in cities?
 2 How do pocket parks help urban communities?
 3 Why are cities unattractive to wildlife?
 4 How can we attract more wildlife to cities?

6 **THINK** Discuss the questions.
 1 Why do you think so many people want to live in cities?
 2 Which ideas from the leaflet could help your local community the most?

Look UP! Look online and find out more about The High Line, New York. What was it before it was a park?

GRAMMAR
First conditional

7 Complete the table with the words *action* and *result*.

Action	1 ....
If we (don't) plant more trees in our cities,	the air quality will/won't improve.
2	3 ....
Cities will/won't attract wildlife	if they (don't) provide water, trees and wildflowers.
Questions	
If more people move into cities, what will happen? 4	
What will happen if more people move into cities? 5	
We use *if* + present simple to talk about the 6 .... and *will* or *won't* + verb to talk about the 7	
If the 8 .... is first, we put a comma after it.	

CHECK IT! ➔ MY GRAMMAR REFERENCE & PRACTICE p110

8 Match 1–4 with A–D to complete the sentences.
 1 If we don't help bees and other insects, ...
 2 Cities will get hotter and more polluted ....
 3 If unused land is turned into pocket parks, ...
 4 It will be easier for people to exercise ....

 A people will feel safer.
 B they won't pollinate our food plants.
 C if we build more parks in our cities.
 D if we don't plant more trees and plants in them.

9 Complete the first conditional sentences with the correct forms of the verbs in brackets.
 1 If we .... (plant) these vegetables now, they .... (be) ready in Autumn.
 2 You .... (not get) fit if you .... (not exercise).
 3 Where .... you .... (walk) your dog if there .... (be not) any green spaces?
 4 If you .... (take) public transport, you .... (create) less pollution.
 5 How .... you .... (feel) if the local park .... (close)?

10 💬 Ask and answer about what you will do in these situations. Use the first conditional.
 1 you can't sleep tonight
 2 there's no internet all weekend
 3 you lose your house keys on the way home
 4 a metre of snow falls tomorrow

 > What will you do if you can't sleep tonight?
 > If I can't sleep tonight, I'll call you for a chat!

PROJECT BUILDER 3

Decide which green projects to include in the Eco Zone of your park.

➔ Workbook **Project Log** p13

11 👥 Look at the list of green projects you could include in your park and think of one more.
 • plant trees
 • plant wildflowers
 • collect and use rain water
 • provide fresh water for animals and birds
 • provide recycling bins

12 Choose three green projects from exercise 11 to include in the Eco Zone of your park. Discuss and write down the benefits of each project.

 > If we plant wildflowers in the Eco Zone, people will enjoy walking there.
 > And there will be more insects.
 > And if there are more insects, other animals will come to eat them!

3.4 OUTDOOR EVENTS

LESSON OBJECTIVES
- Learn outdoor events vocabulary
- Learn about unusual festivals
- Focus on round-up videos

VOCABULARY

1 Match the outdoor events in the box with adverts 1–10.

arts and crafts market	carnival ......
car show	charity football match ......
concert	food (truck) festival ......
funfair	fun run ......
music festival	outdoor cinema ......

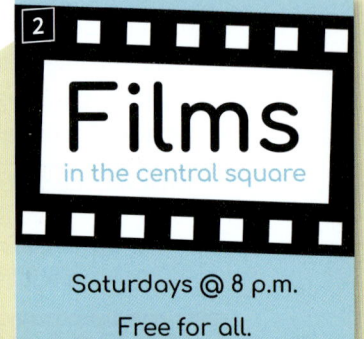

3 48 hours, 25 bands — A weekend you'll never forget — Silverdale campsite

1 Sabrina and the Superstars — Performing live again! — Main stadium 11/08

2 Films in the central square — Saturdays @ 8 p.m. — Free for all.

4 200+ classic cars — FREE ENTRY — Bagshot Farm — 07/07

5 Food from 20 different countries – all parked in the same place! — Metro car park — Saturday 10 a.m.

6 5 km — Enjoyment and exercise for all the family — Run begins at 9 a.m. Sunday Greenhill Forest

7 Join us again this year to dance in the streets of London to celebrate … Caribbean food, music and culture — 25/26 JULY — Notting Hill

8 Rides and attractions for all ages. See beautiful views of the city from the top of our big wheel! — 21–28 August City Park

9 See and buy work by local artists — Claude Street — Sunday 10 a.m.

10 Enjoy the match and raise money! — Teachers vs students Saturday 1 p.m.

2 💬 Discuss the questions.
1 Which of these events are your favourites?
2 What was the last outdoor event you went to? When and where was it?
3 Is there anything about these types of events you don't like?

LISTENING

3 ▶Video Read the *Video focus*. Then watch the first part of the video. What type of round-up video is it? Choose the correct option 1–3, then complete it.
1 Three of the most unusual …
2 Three ways to …
3 Three things you didn't know about …

> **Video FOCUS** **Round-up videos** are a quick and interesting way to present a topic through a list of examples. They often have titles such as 'Three of the most unusual …', 'Four great ways to …' or 'Five things you didn't know about …'. Organizing information in this way helps to keep the videos short and easy for viewers to follow.

4 ▶Video Watch the second part of the video. Number festivals A–C in the order the presenters talk about them.

A International Festival of Wormcharming

B Air Guitar World Championships

C World Bog Snorkelling Championships

5 ▶Video Watch the complete video. Answer the questions.
1 In which country do the Air Guitar World Championships take place?
2 Do competitors play real guitars at the championships?
3 How many people are in each team at the International Festival of Wormcharming?
4 How much time does each team have to catch worms?
5 In which month do the World Bog Snorkelling Championships take place?
6 What must competitors do to win at the World Bog Snorkelling Championships?

6 💬 **THINK** Discuss the questions.
1 Which festival from this lesson would you most / least like to go to? Why?
2 Are there any unusual festivals in your country? What do you know about them?

7 **MEDIATION** Imagine you are at one of the festivals from exercise 4. An English-speaking friend asks you some questions about it in a text message. Write a reply.
1 Where is it?
2 What happens there?
3 Are you enjoying it?

PROJECT BUILDER 4

Create a programme of events for your park's opening weekend.

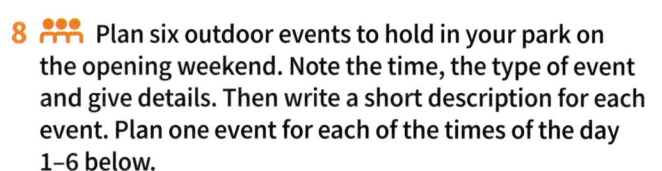

→ Workbook **Project Log** p13

8 👥 Plan six outdoor events to hold in your park on the opening weekend. Note the time, the type of event and give details. Then write a short description for each event. Plan one event for each of the times of the day 1–6 below.
1 Saturday morning
2 Saturday afternoon
3 Saturday evening
4 Sunday morning
5 Sunday afternoon
6 Sunday evening

Time	Event	Details	Description
• Saturday morning • 9 a.m.	Fun run	• all ages • 3 km • all zones • prizes	On Saturday morning at 9 a.m., there will be a fun run for people of all ages. The run is 3 km long and goes through all the zones in the park. Winners will receive great prizes!

3.5 HELP!

LESSON OBJECTIVES • Learn how to ask for and offer help

SPEAKING

1 💬 Look at the photo below. Discuss the questions.
1 What is happening in the photo?
2 Do you like eating outdoors? Why / Why not?

2 ▶ Video Watch the first part of the video. Answer the questions.
1 Why are Lucy and Marcel organizing a picnic?
2 Why is Lucy unhappy with Marcel?
3 What happens to Marcel's earbud?

3 ▶ Video Complete the *Key phrases* with the words in the box. You can use them more than once. Then watch again and check.

| favour | hand | help | manage |

KEY PHRASES
Asking for and offering help

Asking for help
Could you help me, please?
I need your [1] _____, please.
I can't [2] _____ this on my own.
Could you do me a [3] _____?
Could you give me a [4] _____ (with these)?

Offering to help
What can I do to [5] _____?
Do you need a [6] _____ with that?
What else can I do?
Can I help you (with anything else)?
Can you manage?

4 ▶ Video Look at the photo below. What do you think happened next with Marcel's earbud? Then watch the second part of the video and check.

5 🔊 13 Listen to questions 1 and 2. Then choose the correct option to complete the *Pronunciation* rules. Practise saying the questions with the correct intonation.
1 Can I help you with anything else?
2 What can I do to help?

PRONUNCIATION Question intonation
In questions where the answer is *yes* or *no*, the speaker's voice usually goes **up** / **down** at the end.
In questions that ask for information, the speaker's voice usually goes **up** / **down** at the end.

6 🔊 14 Read the *Skill UP!* Then listen to an extract from the video. Which two phrases does Marcel use to agree to help Lucy? _____

Skill UP! Show you are happy to help people when they ask by using the phrases *Sure*, *Of course* and *With pleasure*.

7 💬 You are going to prepare and perform a role-play. Imagine you are organizing a surprise party for a friend. Make a list of food, drinks and other things you need.
Cake, orange juice, party hats …

8 💬 Read the information below, then perform your role-play. Use the *Key phrases* to help you.

Student A You're organizing the party. Ask Student B to help you prepare some of the things on your list.
Student B Offer to help Student A prepare for the party.

> There's a lot to prepare for Maria's surprise party. I can't manage on my own. Could you help me, please?

> Yes, of course. What can I do to help?

40

3.6 WELCOME EVERYONE

LESSON OBJECTIVES • Write a speech • Learn about language and structure in a speech

WRITING

1 Read the list of special events. When do people usually give speeches in your culture? Choose from the list or add your own ideas.
   - An important birthday (e.g. 15, 18, 40)
   - A wedding
   - The birth of a new baby
   - The opening of a new building or facility
   - An awards ceremony
   - When a sports team wins a competition

2 🔊 15 Listen to the beginnings of three speeches. Match each speech 1–3 to a special event from exercise 1.

3 🔊 15 Listen again. What phrases do the speakers use to get people's attention? Which are most and least formal?
   Welcome everyone.

4 🔊 16 Read and listen to the speech. What special event does Jing Wu talk about?

"Ladies and gentlemen, boys and girls, thank you all for coming to our opening ceremony. My name is Jing Wu and I would like to tell you about our brilliant new community leisure centre.

The centre has something for everyone. If you are a family with young children, you will love the fantastic outdoor playground and the safe, fun children's swimming pool.

If you like keeping fit, you will definitely enjoy the large, modern gym and the beautiful sports pool. There will also be fitness classes for teenagers, adults and older adults in the sports hall next to the gym. And if you're hungry after all that exercise, there's a wonderful café with a great menu of healthy and delicious food.

Our opening weekend events include a charity football match at 2 p.m. today, a music festival in the evening, and an outdoor cinema tomorrow afternoon. We also have food trucks and a funfair here all weekend.

We hope that the new leisure centre will bring our community together. We are sure it will help us all stay fit, happy and healthy. Now, please come inside and have a look around. Thank you!"

5 **MEDIATION** A friend doesn't speak English. Summarize the speech from exercise 4 for them.

6 Read the *Skill UP!* Find examples of points 2–5 in the speech in exercise 4. Underline your answers.

Skill UP!

Writing a speech
1 Think about your audience and how formal you want the language in your speech to be.
2 Choose a suitable phrase to get everyone's attention at the beginning.
3 Introduce yourself and say why you are making the speech.
4 Use the pronoun *you* to talk directly to the audience.
5 Use lots of positive adjectives.

7 Add one or two positive adjectives to each sentence. Use the speech in exercise 4 for ideas.
   There's a beautiful lake in our park.
   1 A band will play a concert tonight.
   2 If you're brave, try the skatepark.
   3 Go for a walk in the Eco Zone if you like flowers.
   4 Visit the café if you would like a coffee or a meal.
   5 Every night, we'll show a film at the outdoor cinema.

PROJECT BUILDER 5

Write a speech to give at the opening of your park.

➡ Workbook **Project Log** p14

8 Write a speech to give at the opening ceremony for your park. Work in groups for Part A only.

A Plan
   - Decide which features of your park to mention.
   - Decide how the different groups of users in your community will benefit from the features.
   - Look back at Project Builder 4 and decide which outdoor events from the opening weekend to mention.

B Write
   - Use the tips from the *Skill UP!*
   - Describe the features and facilities in your park with positive adjectives.
   - Say how the park benefits the community.

C Read and check
   - Check that your speech includes all the necessary information.
   - Read it out loud, record it, or film it. How does it sound?

3 PROJECT

Design a park for the whole community

SHARE AND REVIEW

Use your Project Log → p12–14

1. Look back at your Project Builders 1–5 for this unit. Which Project Builder is about:
   - **A** outdoor activities? __2__
   - **B** outdoor events? _____
   - **C** the features of your park? _____
   - **D** the opening ceremony for your park? _____
   - **E** the benefits of green projects? _____

2. Share and review the work from your Project Builders. Is there anything you want to change?

DECIDE

3. Complete the table with your final choices for features and activities in the zones of your park.

Family Zone:	Action Zone:
Quiet Zone:	Eco Zone:

4. Discuss and decide what shape your park will be, e.g. long, wide, square, circular.

CREATE

5. Draw and label your park. Remember to include all four zones in your design.
   - Add labels to the park features. Use your plan from Project Builder 1.
   - Add labels to show what outdoor activities people will do in your park and where. Use your work from Project Builder 2.
   - Add labels to give information about the green projects in your Eco Zone. Use your work from Project Builder 3.
   - Make a copy of your programme of events from Project Builder 4. Put this with your final park design.

42

PRESENT

6 You are going to give your park-opening ceremony speech to the class. First, read the *Project skills*.

PROJECT SKILLS

Giving a group speech or presentation

Before you speak
- Before you give a speech or presentation as a group, decide who will say what.
- Practise together as a group before you present in front of an audience.

During the speech
- Start by getting everyone's attention.
- Make eye contact with some of the people in the audience.
- Speak slowly and clearly.

PROJECT COACH ▶ Video

7 Choose one of your speeches from Project Builder 5. Divide it into sections so each person speaks. Follow the advice in the *Project skills* and give your speech to the class or to another group.

8 Display your park design in the classroom, for example, on a wall or table. Include your programme of events from Project Builder 4. Then walk around the classroom and look at the other groups' park designs. Write down three things you like and one question about each group's design.

9 Give the other groups some feedback and ask your questions. Use the *Key phrases* to help you.

KEY PHRASES

Giving feedback
- I really like this because …
- That's a great idea. We didn't think of that.

Asking questions
- Why did you choose this?
- Who will use / do this?

REFLECT

10 Think about your project work in this unit. Read the statements and choose your reaction.

COLLABORATION
1 Our group can practise and improve a speech together.
☹ 😐 🙂 😊 🤩

CREATIVITY
2 Our group can design an interesting park.
☹ 😐 🙂 😊 🤩

COMMUNICATION
3 Our group can listen carefully to the other groups' speeches.
☹ 😐 🙂 😊 🤩

11 Complete these sentences for you.
1 I am pleased with our park design because ___
2 I want to improve ___

➔ Workbook **Project Log** p15

4 A helping hand

UNIT OBJECTIVES

YOUR PROJECT Record or film a radio interview about helping others

Project Builders 1–5:
1. Choose some good deeds to do.
2. Choose a volunteering opportunity.
3. Choose things to donate to charity.
4. Prepare to talk about how doing good is good for you.
5. Write a formal email to a radio station.

Present your recording or video.

VOCABULARY
- Personality adjectives
- Phrasal verbs

GRAMMAR
- *be going to* for future plans and intentions
- *be going to* and *will* for predictions

LESSON OBJECTIVES • Learn phrases for talking about good deeds • Talk about everyday good deeds

WARM-UP

1 Complete the phrases with the words in the box.

| donate | help | offer | put | volunteer | write |

1 .... (money / clothes) to charity
2 .... your seat to (an older adult) on public transport
3 .... at (an animal shelter)
4 .... (an older adult) across the street
5 .... some litter in the bin
6 .... a thank-you message

2 Match the good deeds in exercise 1 to photos A–F. Can you think of any more good deeds?

3 ▶Video Watch Curtis and Amanda's vlog. Discuss the questions.
1 Why is Curtis doing good deeds?
2 What good deeds does Curtis do or plan to do?
3 Which of these good deeds were in exercise 1?

4 ▶Video Watch again and answer the questions.
1 Why does Curtis donate his jumper to charity?

2 Why does Curtis write a message to Mr Thomas?

3 Why is Amanda unhappy when Curtis calls her?

4 Where does Curtis plan to volunteer?

5 What advice does Curtis give about donating money to charity?

Curtis and Amanda's
VLOG
A day for doing good

PROJECT BUILDER 1 Choose some good deeds to do.

→ Workbook **Project Log** p16

5 Your project is to record or film a radio interview about helping others. Another group will ask the questions and you will answer by talking about your good deeds and the benefits of doing good. Read question 1 below then complete exercises 6 and 7 to help you prepare your answer.

🎤 **Question 1: What good deeds did you do recently and who did they help?**

6 Think about the good deeds from this lesson and discuss the questions.
• Which are easy / more difficult to do?
• Which can you do quickly? Which need more time?
• Which can you do at home or at school?
• Who will the good deed help, e.g. a friend, a family member, or the community?

7 Complete the table with two good deeds for each group member. Then try to do them this week.

Name	Good deeds

45

4.2 VOLUNTEERING

LESSON OBJECTIVES
- Learn about different ways to volunteer
- Learn personality adjectives
- Use *be going to* for future plans and intentions

VOCABULARY

1 THINK Which of these is not a reason to volunteer? Which reasons do you think are the most important?
1. to help other people
2. to get work experience
3. to earn money
4. to meet new people
5. to learn new skills
6. to feel good

2 MEDIATION Work in groups of three. Each read one of the volunteering opportunities on the website. Then tell your group about it in English. Which volunteering opportunity do you think is the most interesting?

Join our team of generous teenage volunteers and do some good in your community

Today's opportunities

Dog shelter helper

YOUR ROLE: To play with, feed, clean and walk dogs; use social media to help find homes for dogs.
YOU: You are hard-working, kind and an animal lover.

Click here to apply

Computer skills trainer

YOUR ROLE: To help older adults improve their skills with the internet, mobile phones, printers, etc.
YOU: You are patient, polite and helpful. You have good communication and IT skills.

Click here to apply

Theatre group performer

YOUR ROLE: To take part in free music and drama performances in children's hospitals, kindergartens and community centres.
YOU: You are confident. You play a musical instrument, can sing, or can act.

Click here to apply

3 Match the adjectives in the box to their opposites from the website.

| impatient | lazy | mean | rude |
| shy | unhelpful | unkind | |

4 🔊 17 Listen and match one adjective from exercise 3 to each of the four speakers.

5 Read Keya and Daniel's messages. Which volunteering role does Keya think will be good for Daniel and why?

Keya So, are you going to volunteer with me in the holidays, or not?

Daniel I'm still not sure. Are Miko and Charlie going to do it too, or is it just you?

Keya Charlie isn't going to do it, but Miko is. We found a great website with volunteering opportunities. I'm going to apply for the role of Dog shelter helper and Miko's going to apply for the Theatre group performer role. They also need a Computer skills trainer. You're good with computers and quite patient and helpful. Would that be good for you?

Daniel That sounds perfect for me.

Keya Miko and I are going to meet at my house at seven o'clock. Are you going to come over, too?

Daniel Yes, I am.

Keya Great. We also need to talk about our final science project. What are we going to do?

Daniel Let's talk about it later. My football match starts in five minutes. See you at 7.

GRAMMAR
be going to for future plans and intentions

6 Find examples of *be going to* in the messages in exercise 5. Then complete the table.

Affirmative		
I'm	going to	apply for the role of Dog shelter helper.
He's / She's / It's		
We're / You're / They're		
Negative		
I'm not		
He / She / It ¹ _____	³ _____	do it.
We / You / They ² _____		
Questions	**Answers**	
⁴ _____ you **going to** come over, too?	Yes, I ⁶ _____. No, I'm not.	
What are we ⁵ _____ do?	Let's talk about it later.	

CHECK IT! ➡ MY GRAMMAR REFERENCE & PRACTICE p112

7 Complete the answers (A) to the questions (Q) using the messages in exercise 5.
1. Q: What are Miko and Keya going to do in the holidays?
   A: They're going to *volunteer*.
2. Q: Is Charlie going to volunteer in the holidays?
   A: No, _____.
3. Q: What role is Miko going to apply for?
   A: He's going to _____.
4. Q: Is Daniel going to go to Keya's house at seven o'clock?
   A: _____, he _____.
5. Q: What are Keya and Daniel planning to talk about later?
   A: _____ going to _____.

8 Complete each sentence with the correct form of *be going to* and the verb in brackets.
1. I _____ (do) some shopping for the older people who live in our apartment block. My dad _____ (come) with me.
2. Nicolas: How _____ (stay) safe while collecting litter?
   Liliana: I _____ (wear) strong shoes and thick gloves.
3. Alex: _____ (you / help) a dog from the shelter?
   Beatrice: Yes, I _____ (keep) it.

9 🔊 18 Read the *Pronunciation*, then listen and repeat sentences 1–3 using *gonna*.

> **PRONUNCIATION** *gonna*
> *Going to* is usually pronounced as one word: *gonna*.
> 1 I'm going to volunteer.
> 2 He's going to help someone.
> 3 We're going to plant some trees.

10 Choose one of the goals below or use your own idea. Write your goal as a sentence and include a time limit. Then write four things you are going to do to achieve it.
I want to get better at basketball by next month.
- *I'm going to practise every day.*
- *I'm going to …*
1 get better at a sport
2 learn a new skill
3 improve my English
4 get fitter and healthier

11 Work in groups of three or four. Read out the four things you are going to do to achieve your goal. Can you guess what your group members' goals are?

PROJECT BUILDER 2

Choose a volunteering opportunity.

➡ Workbook **Project Log** p16

12 Read question 2 of your radio interview, then complete exercises 13–16 to help you prepare your answer.

> 🎙 **Question 2:** Where are you going to volunteer and why did you choose that role?

13 Choose three adjectives from this lesson that describe you.

14 Choose the skills and qualities from the list that describe you. Then add two more of your own ideas.
- good IT skills
- good communication skills
- an animal lover
- can play an instrument
- can sing
- can act

15 Choose a volunteering opportunity from this lesson or use your own idea. Imagine you are going to volunteer in this role in the future. Write three or four sentences about your skills and qualities and what you plan to do in the role.
I have good IT skills and I'm patient. I'm going to volunteer to teach older people about computers. I'm going to teach them how to download apps and how to post photos on social media.

16 👥 Tell your group about your choice from exercise 15.

47

4.3 DONATIONS

LESSON OBJECTIVES
- Read about things you can donate to charity
- Use *be going to* and *will* for predictions

Four things you can donate to charity

We don't all have enough money to donate to charity, but there are lots of things you can give to help other people.

1 Teddy bears

SAFE (Stuffed Animals For Emergencies) is an American organization that collects old teddy bears and other soft toys and gives them to police and firefighters to use in emergencies. When young children are scared, they feel safer with a soft teddy bear to **cuddle**.

2 Socks and blankets

Unfortunately, many homeless people must live, and often sleep, on the streets. When it's **chilly**, they need warm clothes and blankets. Charity organizations say that socks are especially necessary because not many people donate them. New socks are best, but clean, used socks (with no **holes**!) are also very welcome, especially in winter.

3 Gaming equipment

Donate your old gaming equipment to Get Well Gamers UK and they will give it to children's hospitals. Playing video games helps entertain bored young people who are in hospital for a long time. Research also shows gaming can help reduce pain.

4 Glasses

An organization called Lions Clubs International sends used glasses to people around the world. Glasses are often expensive and some families can't **afford** to buy them. Getting a pair for free can completely change someone's life.

READING

1. What kinds of things do people donate to charity?

2. 🔊 19 Look at the photos in the article. Who might need these donated items? Then read, listen and check.
   Homeless people might need the socks and blankets.

3. Answer the questions.
   1. Who do SAFE give the donated soft toys to?
   2. Why do charity organizations want people to donate more socks?
   3. What can people donate to Get Well Gamers UK?
   4. How can video games help people?
   5. What can people donate to Lions Clubs International?
   6. Who do Lions Clubs International send the donations to?

4. Read the *Skill UP!* Then answer the questions to help you guess the meaning of the word *cuddle* from the article.

   Skill UP! When you find a word you don't know, try to guess its meaning by looking at the words around it. For example, here we can use the underlined words to help us understand the word *cuddle*:
   When young children are scared, they feel safer with a soft teddy bear to **cuddle**.

   1. Why are teddy bears soft?
   2. What do young children usually do with teddy bears when they are scared?

5. Now try to guess the meaning of the other words in bold in the article.

6. **MEDIATION** Look online and find three interesting facts about a charity in your local area. Tell the class in English.

GRAMMAR
be going to and *will* for predictions

7 Match underlined sentences A and B from the reader's comment with rules 1 and 2 from the grammar box below.

Readers' comments

Marek_#3
^AThe weather forecast shows it's going to be a very cold winter this year. ^BI think homeless charities will need blankets, strong shoes and warm clothes.

be going to and will for predictions
1. We use *will* to make predictions based on what we believe or know. _____
2. We use *be going to* to make predictions based on what we can see / hear / smell / feel. _____
   what we see = black clouds   prediction = It's going to rain.

CHECK IT! → MY GRAMMAR REFERENCE & PRACTICE p112

8 Match sentences 1 and 2 with A and B in each pair.
1. 1 A Dad will get tired soon.
   2 B Dad is going to get tired soon.
   A He always gets tired at this time on Friday evenings.
   B It's nearly midnight and he's still working.
2. 1 ___ She'll win.
   2 ___ She's going to win.
   A She's first in the race and close to the finish line.
   B She always wins the race.
3. 1 ___ He'll miss the bus.
   2 ___ He's going to miss the bus.
   A He's always late.
   B He's running, but the bus is already leaving.
4. 1 ___ It's going to be delicious.
   2 ___ It'll be delicious.
   A He's a great cook. Everything he makes is delicious.
   B It smells great.

9 Complete the sentences with the correct form of *be going to* or *will* and the verbs in brackets.
1. I'm sure you _____ (feel) better soon.
2. It's a job for two people. You _____ (not manage) on your own.
3. He's driving too fast. He _____ (crash).
4. We _____ (not go) skiing because there isn't any snow.

10 Complete the sentences. Make them true for you.
1. The weather today looks _____, so after school I'm going to _____.
2. I'm good at _____, so I'll _____ one day.
3. I can't stand _____, so I definitely won't _____.
4. My best friend is _____, so he / she will _____ when he / she is older.

11 Work in groups of four or more and follow the instructions.
1. Fold your pieces of paper from exercise 10 in half so that they all look the same. Then mix them up.
2. One of you choose a piece of paper. If you choose your own piece of paper, put it back and take a different one. Read out the sentences.
3. The rest of the group must listen and try to guess which person in the group wrote the sentences. If you hear your own sentences, don't say it's you!

PROJECT BUILDER 3
Choose things to donate to charity.

→ Workbook **Project Log** p17

12 Read question 3 of your radio interview, then complete exercise 13 to help you prepare your answer.

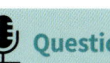

> **Question 3:** What are you planning to donate to charity and how will the items help?

13 What do you have at home that you could donate? As a group, think of six items, then complete the table. Use the list of categories below to help.
- books
- clothes
- electronics
- games
- glasses
- toys

Item	Who will want it?	How will it help?
a winter coat	a homeless person	It's going to be very cold this winter. The coat will keep them warm.

49

4.4 FEELING GOOD ABOUT DOING GOOD

LESSON OBJECTIVES
- Discover how doing good is good for you
- Focus on joining video calls
- Learn phrasal verbs

LISTENING

1 Complete the quiz. Are the sentences true (T) or false (F)?

Test your knowledge with our quick quiz.

Does doing good do you good?

1 Talking over someone's problems with them makes you feel more stressed. .... T / F
2 Doing a good deed once a week makes you feel happier. .... T / F
3 Being kind to others helps you feel more confident. .... T / F
4 Doing good deeds can make your body healthier. .... T / F
5 Volunteering regularly can help you live longer. .... T / F

2 ▶ Video Watch the video and check your answers to the quiz.

3 Read the *Video focus*. How do you say the words in bold in your language?

Video FOCUS

Before you join a video call, remember these tips:
1 Ask people around you not to **disturb** you.
2 Make sure the room you are in is not too light or dark.
3 Think about what other callers will see through your camera.
4 Learn how to switch your camera and **microphone** on and off.
5 Learn how to control digital **backgrounds** and other special effects.
6 **Mute** your other **devices** during the call.

4 ▶ Video Watch again. Which tips from the *Video focus* didn't Professor Perkins follow?

LIFE SKILLS We all make mistakes. Often, a mistake is an opportunity to learn something new or change your behaviour. Think of a time you learned from a mistake. What happened and what did you learn?

5 **MEDIATION** Imagine a friend who doesn't speak English asks you for advice on taking part in video calls. With your partner, give your friend some advice in your own language. Use the *Video focus* to help.

VOCABULARY

6 ▶Video Complete the extracts from the video with the correct form of the phrasal verbs in the box. Then watch again and check.

find out	go away	look after	look at
pick up	take part in	talk over	turn off
turn on	work out		

1 This week, we're going to _____ how doing good is good for us.
2 Professor Perkins, we can't hear you. Please _____ your microphone.
3 When we help a friend _____ their problems, for example, we also feel less stressed.
4 It's very bright, Professor Perkins. Could you _____ the light?
5 After we do something kind, such as _____ the neighbour's cat, or _____ some litter, we get a nice positive feeling.
6 Another study _____ 11–14-year-olds who regularly help others.
7 Oh no! What happened? How do I make that _____?
8 The researchers tested the helpers' blood and found that they were healthier than other students who didn't _____ the research.
9 American scientists also _____ that people who regularly volunteer have a better chance of living longer. This is because volunteering reduces stress.

7 Complete the sentences with the correct form of the phrasal verbs from exercise 6. Use one of the phrasal verbs twice.

1 If you can't _____ the meaning of a new word, look in a dictionary to _____ what it means.
2 Ask the doctor to _____ your knee. She'll probably give you some medicine to make the pain _____.
3 Please _____ your mobile phone during the exam. Do not _____ your phone until you leave the school building.
4 I need to _____ a problem I have at school. Will you help me _____ what to do?
5 Will you _____ our eco-day this weekend? We're going to _____ litter in the local community.

8 💬 Work in small groups. Follow the instructions to complete the challenges.

1 Name five things you need to turn on to make them work.

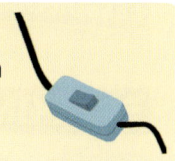

2 Find out the birthdays of the people in your group. Then work out who is the oldest.

3 Name three places where people need to turn off their mobile phones.

4 Find out what clubs or events the people in your group are taking part in at school this year.

PROJECT BUILDER 4

Prepare to talk about how doing good is good for you.

➡ Workbook **Project Log** p17

9 Read question 4 of your radio interview, then complete exercises 10 and 11 to help you prepare your answer.

🎤 **Question 4:** How is doing good good for you?

10 Write answers to the questions. How does doing good help:
1 your mental health?
2 your physical health?
3 you live longer?

11 👥 Compare your answers with the other members of your group.

> For number 1, I wrote that doing good makes you feel less stressed. For example, if you talk over a friend's problems …

51

4.5 TALK IT OVER

LESSON OBJECTIVES • Ask for, give and react to advice • Use phrases that give you time to think

SPEAKING

1 Work in small groups. Discuss the questions.
 1 Are you good at giving advice?
 2 Who can young people talk to if they need advice?

2 ▶Video Watch the first part of the video. Answer the questions.
 1 What did Lucy post on social media?
 2 Why is Alessia's mum angry with Lucy?
 3 What advice does Marcel give Lucy?

3 ▶Video Read the *Key phrases*, then watch again. Tick the phrases they use.

KEY PHRASES
Asking for, giving and reacting to advice

Asking for advice

What do you think I should do?
Have you got any advice?
What do you suggest (doing / I do)?

Giving advice

I (don't) think you should …
You could …
Why don't you … ?

Reacting to advice

I'm not sure that's a good idea.
That's great advice, thanks.
I'll try that, thanks.

4 ▶Video Look at the photo. Why do you think Lucy is unhappy? Watch the second part of the video and check.

5 💬 Read the *Skill UP!* Then follow instructions 1–3 below.

Skill UP! Use these phrases if you need time to think before you answer a question:
Hmm. That's a good question.
Well, let me see.
OK, let me think.

1 Choose a problem from the list below or use your own ideas.
 • You wrote a negative comment about someone online when you were angry and now you feel bad about it.
 • Someone shared a photo of you online that you don't like.
 • Someone wrote something unkind about you online.
2 Work together to think of some good advice for the problem.
3 Write and practise a role-play using language from this lesson. Include one of the phrases from the *Skill UP!*

Student A Explain your problem, ask for advice, then react to the advice you get from your partner.

Student B Listen to your partner's problem and offer them some advice.

4.6 REQUEST FOR AN INTERVIEW

LESSON OBJECTIVES • Write a formal email • Learn about writing a formal email, letter or message

WRITING

1 Who do people usually write formal emails to? Choose two options from the box.

> companies and organizations   friends and family
> people we don't know   people we know well

2 Read Ingrid's email and answer the questions.
1. Why is she writing?
2. How did Ingrid and her classmates decide to help their friends and neighbours?
3. Why does she think listeners will be interested?

To: sarah_cook@community-radio
From: ingrid_nielson@123mail.co.uk
Subject: ¹Can we do an interview?

²Hi there,

³I'm Ingrid and I'm 13. ⁴Just a quick email to ask if my classmates and I could come on the Morning Show and talk about our project to clean up the local community.

As part of our English course at school, our teacher asked us to think of ways to help our friends and neighbours. There is a lot of litter in our neighbourhood so we decided to clean it up.

We would like to come on your show and talk to you about what we did. We think your listeners will be interested to hear from young people trying to make a difference in their community.

⁵Will you help us?

⁶I can't wait to hear from you. ⁷Thanks.

⁸Bye for now,
Ingrid Nielson

---

3 Match the underlined informal phrases in Ingrid's email 1–8 with the more formal phrases A–H.
A ____ Please let me know if you are able to help.
B ____ My name is Ingrid Nielson and I am 13 years old.
C ____ Yours sincerely,
D ____ Dear Ms Cook,
E ____ Thank you.
F ____ I hope to hear from you soon.
G ____ I am writing …
H ____ Request for an interview

4 Read the Skill UP! and choose the correct option.

> **Skill UP!**
> **Writing a formal email, letter or message**
> 1 **Fill in / Don't fill in** the 'subject' box with a short phrase (emails only).
> 2 **Start / Don't start** with Dear plus the correct title, e.g. Mr, Mrs or Ms, and the person's surname.
> 3 **Introduce / Don't introduce** yourself in the first paragraph.
> 4 **Say / Don't say** why you are writing in the first paragraph.
> 5 **Use / Don't use** contractions, e.g. I am not I'm.
> 6 **Use / Don't use** exclamation marks (!) or emojis (☺).
> 7 **Use / Don't use** short forms, e.g. Thanks not Thank you.
> 8 **Finish / Don't finish** with a formal sign-off, e.g. Kind regards or Yours sincerely.

5 Change the sentences to make them more formal.
1. Hello Mr Parker!
2. I'm John and I'm a pupil at Grange School.
3. I want to ask for your help.
4. Will you come to the school event?
5. Write back soon!
6. Thanks and bye.

PROJECT BUILDER 5

Write a formal email to a radio station.

→ Workbook **Project Log** p18

6 Write a formal email to one of the local radio stations below. Ask if you can come on a show and talk about your project from this unit. Work in groups for Part A only.

A Plan
- Why are you writing?
- What is your project about?
- Why will listeners be interested in your project?

B Write
- Follow the tips in the Skill UP! and write your email.

C Read and check
- Check that your email has a formal style.
- Check your spelling and grammar.

RADIO CITY CHAT
New music, local news, listeners' calls
Contact: David Night   david_night@radio-city

Youth Radio
For young people, by young people.
Music, news and issues.
Contact: Selma Miles
selma_miles@youth-radio

53

4 PROJECT

Record or film a radio interview about helping others

SHARE AND REVIEW

Use your Project Log → p16–18

1. 👥 Look back at your Project Builders 1–5 for this unit. Check that you have:
   - a list of good deeds that you did.
   - your plans for volunteering work.
   - a list of six things that you could donate to charity.
   - some reasons why doing good is good for you.

2. 👥 Share and review the work from your Project Builders. Is there anything you want to change?

DECIDE

3. 👥 Read the interview questions in the boxes below and prepare your responses.
   - Make sure all the members of the group will speak.
   - Use Project Builder 5 to help you with the introduction.
   - Use Project Builders 1–4 to answer questions 1–4.

Introduction
"Welcome to the show. Recently, you wrote an email to the radio station. Please could you introduce yourselves, then tell us about your email and why you're here today."

Question 1
"What good deeds did you do recently and who did they help?"

Question 2
"Where are you going to volunteer and why did you choose that role?"

Question 3
"What are you planning to donate to charity and how will the items help?"

Question 4
"How is doing good good for you?"

CREATE

4 Read the *Project skills*. Then practise your interview. Use the *Key phrases* below to give and respond to feedback while practising.

PROJECT SKILLS — Practising in groups
- Listen carefully to the other members of your group while they are practising. Are they speaking slowly and clearly?
- Be honest, but respectful, when giving feedback to each other.
- Help each other with your English, but remember that it doesn't need to be perfect.
- Practise until all members of the group feel confident.

KEY PHRASES

Giving feedback
- It was great when you …
- I noticed that you (spoke a bit too fast).
- Maybe you could (speak more clearly).

Responding to feedback
- Yes, you're right.
- OK, I'll try that, thanks.
- I'm not sure. I think it was OK.

5 Find another group to work with. Group As ask the interview questions and Group Bs answer. Record or film the interview. Then change roles.

Group As:
- Welcome the radio listeners at the beginning.
- Ask Group B to introduce themselves and explain their project (see exercise 3).
- Take turns asking the questions from exercise 3, as well as any other questions you think of.
- Listen carefully and respond positively to what Group B says.

PRESENT

6 Show your recording or video to the rest of the class.

7 Give feedback to each of the groups on their recording or video. Use the *Key phrases* above to help.

PROJECT COACH ▶ Video

REFLECT

8 Think about your project work in this unit. Read the statements and choose your reaction.

COLLABORATION
1 Our group can give respectful feedback and respond to it.
☹ 😐 🙂 😊 🤩

CREATIVITY
2 Our group can record or film an interview.
☹ 😐 🙂 😊 🤩

COMMUNICATION
3 Our group can speak slowly and clearly in an interview.
☹ 😐 🙂 😊 🤩

9 Complete these sentences for you.
1 I am pleased with our radio interview because _____
2 I want to improve _____

➔ Workbook **Project Log** p19

5 Let's play

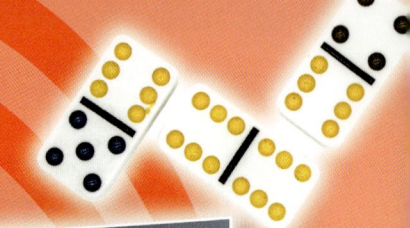

UNIT OBJECTIVES

YOUR PROJECT Make a set of games and challenges

Project Builders 1–5:
1. Prepare a revision word game.
2. Write a set of fun challenges.
3. Create a memory game.
4. Create a wordsearch puzzle.
5. Write an online advert for a games club.

Give your set of games and challenges to another group to play and review.

VOCABULARY
- Senses
- Gaming verbs

GRAMMAR
- can / can't, could / couldn't
- Comparative and superlative adverbs

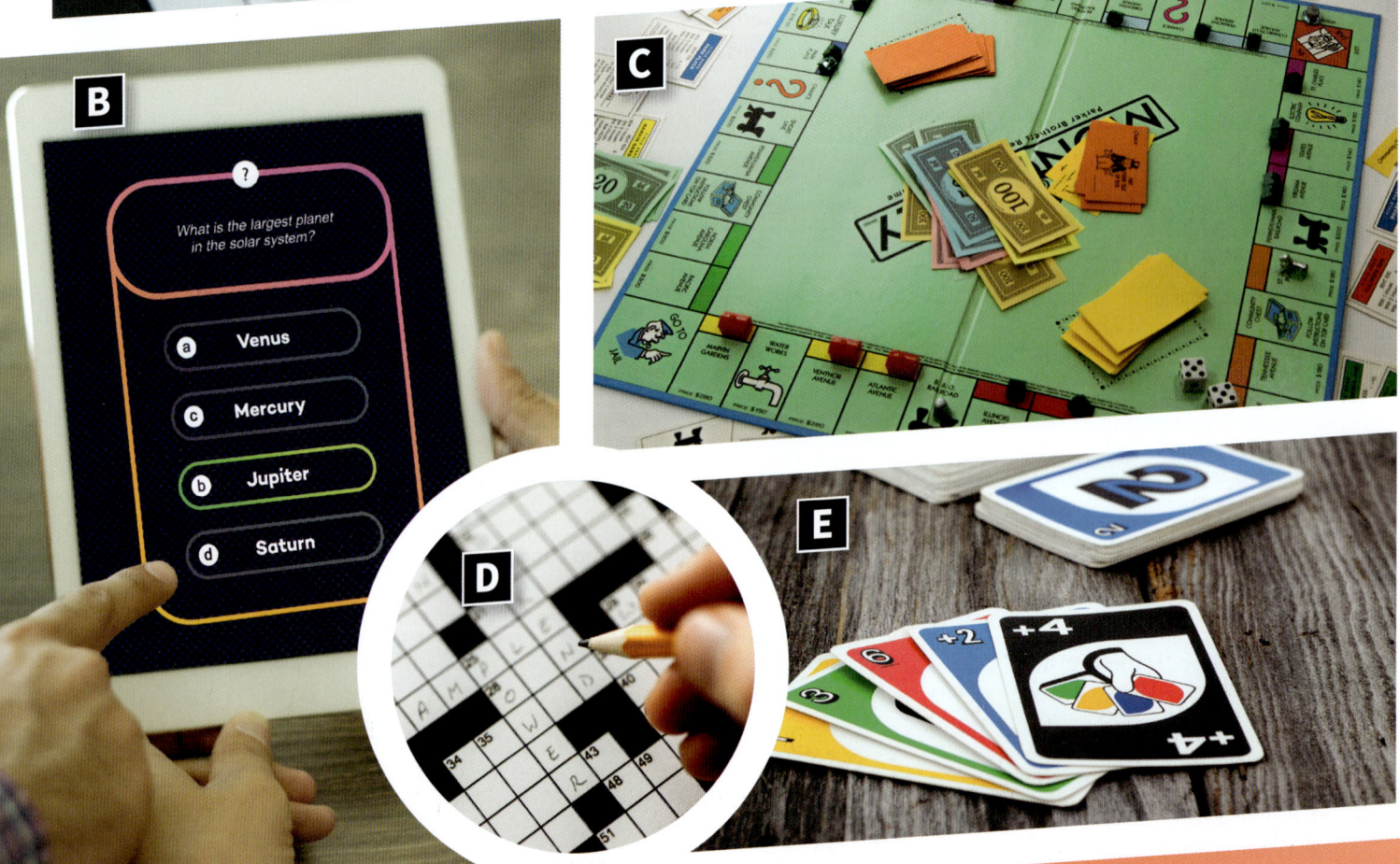

LESSON OBJECTIVES
- Talk about games and the skills you need for them
- Learn games and gaming skills vocabulary

WARM-UP

1 Match the types of games 1–5 to photos A–E.
  1 ____ quiz games   2 ____ word games   3 ____ board games   4 ____ role-playing games   5 ____ card games

2 💬 Discuss the questions.
  1 Which types of games do you play at home or school?
  2 Who do you play with?
  3 What are your favourite games?

3 ▶Video Watch Curtis and Amanda's vlog. Which types of games from exercise 1 does each character like?
  - Amanda ____
  - Curtis ____
  - Sarah ____

Curtis and Amanda's VLOG
Welcome to the games club!

4 What do these words mean in your language?
  1 luck / speed
  2 knowledge / memory
  3 strategy / experience
  4 thought / vocabulary
  5 imagination / patience

5 ▶Video Match the pairs of words 1–5 in exercise 4 with the types of games from exercise 1. Then watch again and check.

6 Choose the correct option.
  1 I don't have enough **patience** / **experience** to play games that take hours and hours. I get bored easily!
  2 My **memory** / **imagination** is very good. I don't usually forget things.
  3 I don't like playing card games. I think you need more **vocabulary** / **luck** than skill to play them, and I prefer games of skill.
  4 I like games where **speed** / **thought** is important because they're exciting. I find slow games boring.
  5 I'm not good at quiz games. I don't have enough general **strategy** / **knowledge**.

7 💬 Are the sentences in exercise 6 true for you? Compare your answers with a partner.

PROJECT BUILDER 1 Prepare a revision word game.

➡ Workbook **Project Log** p20

8 Look back at the vocabulary in Units 1–4 of your Student Book and choose one word for each of the categories below. Make sure the words aren't too easy.
  - useful nouns
  - useful phrasal verbs
  - useful verbs
  - words from this page
  - words I find difficult to remember

9 👥 Check that all the members of the group have different words.

10 Write definitions for your words in English.
  quiz games: games where people answer questions to test their knowledge and memory

57

5.2 CHALLENGES

LESSON OBJECTIVES
- Learn vocabulary related to senses
- Use *can / can't* and *could / couldn't* to talk about ability and permission

VOCABULARY

1 Read the web page. Complete the tasks in sections 1–3.

HOME BLOG ACTIVITIES MORE!

#Amazing You

If you have a few minutes and nothing to do, you'll love our activities page!

1 Body Tricks

Some lucky people are really talented – a beautiful **voice**, fantastic at sports, an amazing brain, and so on. But there are some things that only a few very special people can do. What about you?

- Can you raise one eyebrow? (Most people can do this with practise.)
- Can you roll your tongue? (60% of people can do this.)
- Can you move your ears up and down without moving your face? (Only 10–20% of people can do this.)
- Can you touch your **nose** with your tongue? (Around 10% of people can do this.)

Yes, I can 🙂
No, I can't 🙁

2 Do You Believe Your Eyes?

Human sight is amazing, but it is possible to trick it. Check out these interesting images.
Can you see the **pattern** moving?

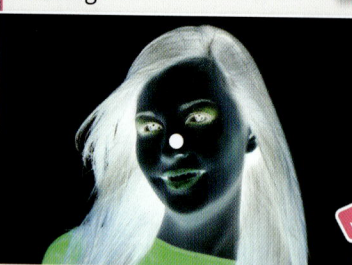

Stare at the dot on the girl's face for 30 seconds then look at a **smooth** white wall or piece of white paper. What can you see?

3 Amazing People Puzzle

Can you work out where the missing numbers go?

| 1 | 6 | 16 | 23 |

Check your answers below!

Could you walk when you were ¹____? Most children start walking around this time, but Freya Minter from the UK could walk when she was just ²____ months old! Her parents couldn't believe it when she took her first steps.

How many languages can you speak? Timothy Doner, from the UK, could speak ³____ languages by the time he was ⁴____ years old … and this amazing teenager learned them without a teacher!

Extra Bubblegum Challenge

"Can I have some bubblegum, Mum?"
"No, you can't!"

My mum told me I couldn't have bubblegum when I was a child. Maybe that's why I love it so much now! If you like **soft**, **sweet** bubblegum, you will love this challenge!

Step 1: Stand in a circle with your friends.
Step 2: Make sure each person has a piece of bubblegum in their **mouth**.
Step 3: Count to three, then see who can blow the biggest bubble!

The world record for a bubblegum bubble is 50.8 cm wide!

2 Complete the table with the highlighted words from the web page.

Hearing	Sight	Smell	Taste	Touch
voice				

Section 3 answers: (1) 1; (2) 6; (3) 23; (4) 16

GRAMMAR

can / can't, could / couldn't

3 Match the underlined examples of *can / could* from the web page on page 58 with descriptions A–D.
- A present ability
- B past ability
- C present permission
- D past permission

4 Complete the table. Use verbs from the web page on page 58.

Affirmative and negative	
I / He / She / It / We / You / They	**can / can't** [1] _____ one eyebrow.
	could / couldn't [2] _____ bubblegum.
Questions	
Can you [3] _____ your tongue?	
Could you [4] _____ when you were one?	

We [5] **use / don't use** *to* after *can* and *could*.

CHECK IT! ➔ MY GRAMMAR REFERENCE & PRACTICE p114

5 Choose the correct option.
1. My cousin **can / can't** put his foot behind his head! He showed me this morning.
2. I **can't / couldn't** play the drums very often when I was living with my parents. They were too loud.
3. **Can / Could** you do the *Renegade* TikTok dance?
4. Ama **can / could** skateboard when she was five.
5. Isre and Emre **can / could** stay here until 7 p.m. Then we'll drive them home for dinner.

6 Complete the text with *can / can't* or *could / couldn't*. Then match gaps 1–6 with descriptions A–D.

#Read My Lips Challenge

When I was ten years old, I was ill and I [1] _____ hear for almost a week. My mum said I [2] _____ stay off school. After a few days at home, I was bored so I tried to learn to read my parents' lips! It was very difficult and I [3] _____ do it very well. Try the **Read My Lips Challenge** and you'll see what I mean!

Step 1: Choose some well-known words from a song, a famous line from a film or TV show, or a sentence in a foreign language.
Step 2: Say the words without sound. You [4] _____ move your lips, but you [5] _____ make any noise.
Step 3: [6] _____ your friends guess what you're saying?

7 💬 **MEDIATION** A friend doesn't speak English. With your partner, explain steps 1–3 of the *Read My Lips Challenge* in your own language.

8 🔊 **20** Read the *Pronunciation*, then listen. Can you hear the strong and weak forms of *can* and *could*? Listen again and repeat.

PRONUNCIATION Strong and weak forms of *can* and *could*

	Strong form	Weak form
can	/kæn/	/kən/
could	/kʊd/	/kəd/

9 Write four sentences about ability and permission. Compare what you could or couldn't do when you were five years old with what you can or can't do now. Use the ideas in the box.

> eat chocolate every day   make your own dinner
> ride a bike   sit in the front seat of a car
> speak English   stay up late   swim   use a laptop
> walk to school on your own

> When I was five years old, I couldn't swim, but now I can.

> Now I can walk to school on my own, but when I was five years old, I couldn't.

10 💬 Use the ideas from the box in exercise 9 to ask and answer questions about past and present abilities and permission with a partner.

> Could you swim when you were five years old?

> Yes, I could. Could you walk to school on your own?

> No, I couldn't, but I can now.

PROJECT BUILDER 2

Write a set of fun challenges.

➔ Workbook **Project Log** p20

11 👥 Try some more challenges. Say what you can and can't do.
1. Can you close your eyes and write a sentence in English?
2. Can you remember ten new words from this lesson? (You can't look at the book while you're doing it!)
3. Can you sing part of a song in English?

12 👥 Write five fun challenges. Invent your own or use ideas from this lesson. Write a question with *Can you … ?* for each challenge.

5.3 MEMORY

LESSON OBJECTIVES
- Learn how to remember things more easily
- Understand pronouns • Use comparative and superlative adverbs

READING

1 How good is your memory? What kind of things do you sometimes forget?

2 Look at the photo of Timur Gareyev. What do you think he is doing? Read lines 1–7 of the blog and check.

3 🔊 21 Now read and listen to the complete blog. What will Omar's tips help readers to do?

4 Complete the statements with one or two words from the blog.
   1 Timur Gareyev has a great _____.
   2 Gareyev played his blindfold chess games while riding an _____.
   3 Omar looked _____ for tips on how to improve his memory.
   4 On school nights, Omar now goes to bed _____ than he did before.
   5 Not long ago, Omar won a _____ at school.

5 Read Omar's notes for his blog. Match topics 1–5 with A–E.

Topics	Tips
1 Sugar	A This helps. Do it regularly.
2 Sleep	B Read them out loud.
3 Exercise	C Avoid it. Eat healthily.
4 Learning study notes	D Teach them to someone else.
5 Remembering facts	E Get enough of this. Do it after you learn something new.

6 💬 **MEDIATION** Explain Omar's tips to your partner in English using the notes above. Then change roles.

7 **THINK** Which of Omar's tips do you think is most useful?

8 Read the *Skill UP!* Then answer the questions.

> **Skill UP!** We use pronouns (e.g. *it, they, them, this, that*) to avoid repeating nouns and noun phrases. When you see one in a text, think about which noun or noun phrase it refers to.

   1 Which noun phrase does *them* in line 7 refer to?
   games of blindfold chess
   2 Which noun does *it* in line 22 refer to?
   3 Which noun does *them* in line 25 refer to?
   4 Which noun phrase does *this* in line 27 refer to?

Omar's blog

About   New posts

1 I enjoy chess, but I play it badly. Normal chess is a difficult game, so can you imagine how difficult blindfold chess is? In blindfold chess, the better player covers their eyes and has to remember where all the pieces are. In 2016, a chess
5 master called Timur Gareyev played 48 games of blindfold chess at the same time, while riding an exercise bike! He won 35 of them. What a fantastic memory he has!

Timur Gareyev

After I heard about Gareyev, I decided to improve my memory. Here are some of the most interesting tips I read
10 online and some of the changes I made:

Fact: Research shows that sugar is bad for your memory and getting enough sleep is very important for it.

Change: I eat more healthily than before and, from Monday to Thursday, try to go to bed earlier than I did.
15 Apparently, sleeping after you learn something new helps you remember it more easily! (Tell the teacher that next time you fall asleep in class!)

Fact: Studies show that exercise is helpful for improving your memory.

20 **Change:** I exercise more regularly than before and can run further. Last week, I ran the fastest out of everyone in a race at school. I'm not sure if it is helping my memory, but I certainly feel happy and healthy. Maybe this is why Gareyev rode that exercise bike!

25 **Fact:** Reading study notes out loud helps you learn them better than reading them in your head.

Change: I tried this and it works! I also read that teaching facts to someone makes them easier to remember.

Why not try some of these tips? Maybe one day you will have a memory like Timur Gareyev's!

60

GRAMMAR
Comparative and superlative adverbs

9 Find an adjective and an adverb in the underlined language in Omar's blog. Then answer the questions.
1 What type of words do we use to describe nouns? ....
2 What type of words do we use to describe verbs, and say how we do things? ....
3 How do we form regular adverbs? ....

10 Complete the table with examples of adverbs from Omar's blog.

	Adjective	Adverb	Comparative adverb	Superlative adverb
1 Adverbs ending in -ly	healthy	healthily	1	the most healthily
2 Adverbs that take the same form as adjectives	fast	fast	faster	2 ....
3 Irregular adverbs	good	well	3	the best
	bad	4	worse	the worst

CHECK IT! → MY GRAMMAR REFERENCE & PRACTICE p114

11 Find four more adverbs in Omar's blog. Match them to rows 1, 2 or 3 from the table in exercise 10.

12 Choose the correct option.
1 I eat **more healthily** / **the most healthily** out of everyone in my family and I remember things **well** / **better** than everyone else!
2 Kelly did **worse** / **the worst** than me on the English test today. She said she wasn't feeling well and her memory was working **more slowly** / **the most slowly** than usual!
3 I read **slower** / **the most slowly** out of all my classmates, but I can do maths **more quickly** / **the quickest** than most of them.

13 Complete the sentences so they are true for you. Then compare with a partner.
I swim well.
1 I .... well.
2 I can .... easily.
3 I .... worse than my best friend, but they .... worse than me.
4 I .... the worst out of all my friends.
5 I can .... faster than my mum / dad, but she / he can .... better than me.
6 I .... better than my mum / dad, but she / he .... better than me.

14 Complete the text with adverbs in the correct form. Use the adjectives in brackets.

The members of our group are all good at different things. Jan is a great musician. He can sing ^{1}............ (beautiful) than everyone else. Aga is a brilliant swimmer and can swim ^{2}............ (far) in our group. Sonia is brilliant at IT. She understands computers ^{3}............ (good) than anyone I know. We all work ^{4}............ (hard) at English, but Alexi speaks it ^{5}............ (good) because his mum is English.

15 Play a memory game in groups of three or four. Read the paragraph in exercise 14 for two minutes then cover it. Try to remember and say as many of the details from the paragraph as you can. Use the picture grid to help you.

Jan (M)
Aga (F)
Sonia (F)
Alexi (M)

> Jan is a great musician. He sings more beautifully than everyone else. Aga …

PROJECT BUILDER 3
Create a memory game.
→ Workbook **Project Log** p21

16 Talk about your skills and abilities using comparative and superlative adverbs.

> Dylan is a great cook. He cooks better than everyone else in the group.

> You're really good at running, Julia. You can run the fastest out of our group.

17 Write a paragraph like the one in exercise 14 about the skills and abilities of the members of your group.

18 Create a picture grid like the one in exercise 15.

61

5.4 GAMING

LESSON OBJECTIVES
- Listen to teenagers talking about gaming
- Learn gaming verbs
- Learn to listen for examples

LISTENING

1 💬 Discuss the questions about video games. Compare your answers.
1. Do you play video games? How often?
2. Do you think playing video games is good for you? Why / Why not?

2 🔊 22 Listen to two teenagers talking about their gaming habits and attitudes. Number questions A–D in the order that they answer them.
A ...... Do you think that teenagers spend too much time playing video games?
B ...... Which devices (e.g. phone, console, computer) do you use to play video games?
C ...... Are some games too violent?
D ...... Which are your favourite video games or types of video games?

3 🔊 22 Read the *Skill UP!* Then listen again. Complete the sentences below with the types of games from the box.

> **Skill UP!** We use *for example*, *like* and *such as* to introduce examples. Listen for these. They can help you follow a speaker's main points.

| adventure games | driving games | fighting games |
| simple games |

1. Kyle likes ....
2. Chantelle likes ....
3. Kyle prefers to play .... on his phone.
4. Chantelle prefers to play .... in the car.

VOCABULARY

4 How do you say the verbs in the box in your language?

avoid	balance	beat	collect	compete
continue	control	dislike	hurt	recognize
solve	worry

5 🔊 23 Choose the correct option to complete the extracts from the audio in exercises 2 and 3. Then listen and check.
1. I like games where you have to **collect** / **compete** useful things, discover clues, **solve** / **recognize** puzzles and **worry** / **avoid** danger.
2. I like to **compete** / **balance**, for example, in fighting games. I like to **beat** / **avoid** the other players' scores.
3. That's not something I **hurt** / **worry** about really. I think most teenagers can **control** / **dislike** how much gaming they do.
4. It can be hard to **control** / **balance** gaming with the other things I need to do, such as my homework or exercise. Often, I just want to **avoid** / **continue** playing.
5. Perhaps, but I **dislike** / **worry** violent games anyway. I prefer to play *with* other players than to fight *against* them.
6. I **recognize** / **solve** the difference between gaming and reality. I would never **hurt** / **collect** anyone in real life.

62

6 Read the introduction to the quiz. What does it say about gaming and English?

GAMING ENGLISH presents ...
Let's go!
A Quiz for Gamers

It's official! Swedish research suggests that gaming is a great way to improve your English. Many frequent gamers are also keen language learners. They often have better English than non-gamers. But how good is your knowledge of gaming English? Test your skills in our multiple-choice quiz. Let's go!

1 What do the letters *AFK* mean?
   A About fifty kilobytes
   B Away from keyboard
   C Ask for knowledge

2 In gaming, what is a *bug*?
   A a dangerous enemy
   B a puzzle you must solve
   C a mistake in the design of a game

3 A *noob, newb* or *noobie* is a player who is:
   A not very experienced.
   B as good as the others on their team.
   C not as interested in the game as the others in the team.

4 If a player is *toxic*, they:
   A avoid other players.
   B are rude to other players.
   C worry too much about losing.

5 If a player is *salty*, they:
   A are less skilful than the other members of their team.
   B have a slow computer.
   C are disappointed and upset.

7 Choose the correct option A–C to complete the quiz. Check your answers at the bottom of the page.

8 💬 Do you know any other gaming words in English?

9 **THINK** Why do you think frequent gamers often have better English than non-gamers?

> ✓ To compare two things that are the same we can say:
> *Hannah is **as** skilful **as** Scott at video games.*
> To compare two things that are different, we can say:
> *Charlie is**n't as** skilful **as** Scott. / Charlie is **less** skilful **than** Scott.*

PROJECT BUILDER 4
Create a wordsearch puzzle.
➔ Workbook **Project Log** p21

10 👥 Race the other members of your group to find four words from exercise 4 in the wordsearch puzzle.

11 Create a wordsearch puzzle using eight words from exercise 4.

V	S	C	F	Q	A	T
A	V	O	I	D	I	V
J	I	N	L	M	L	A
W	B	T	G	V	L	W
Y	R	R	O	W	E	E
H	T	O	H	O	N	B
B	A	L	A	N	C	E

Quiz answers: 1B, 2C, 3A, 4B, 5C

63

5.5 IT'S ONLY A GAME …

LESSON OBJECTIVES
- Interact during games and activities
- Learn how to ask, explain or check something during a game

SPEAKING

1 Do you agree with statements 1–3?
1 Taking part in a game is more important than winning.
2 When playing a game, you should always try to win.
3 I am a competitive person.

2 Compare your answers to exercise 1. Who is more competitive?

3 THINK How is competing with other people good or bad for us? Think about the topics in the box.

| games   money   popularity   sports   tests and exams |

LIFE SKILLS Losing at sports and games can be difficult, especially if you are competitive. How can you be a 'good loser' and why is it important?

4 Video Watch the first part of the video. Who is the most competitive person, Amy, Lucy or Marcel?

5 Video Watch again. Answer the questions.
1 How many cards does each player get at the start of the game?
2 How long do players have to complete the challenge on the card?
3 How do the characters decide who goes first?

6 Video Complete the *Key phrases* with the words in the box. Then watch again and check.

| better   deal   do   done   ready   roll   shall   timer |

KEY PHRASES
Interacting during games and activities

Talking about the rules	Talking about taking turns
What do we have to [1]_____ ? Let's check the instructions / rules. Sorry, that's against the rules.	Is everyone [5]_____ ? (It's) my / your turn. I'm / You're next. [6]_____ we play again?

Talking about stages of a game	Reacting during the game
Set up the board. [2]_____ the cards. [3]_____ the dice. Move your counter. Start the [4]_____ . Time's up!	Well [7]_____ !/ Lucky you! / You win! Hard luck. / [8]_____ luck on your next turn. That's not fair!

7 Video Look at the photo. What do you think happened when Lucy got up to answer the door? Watch the second part of the video and check.

8 Read the *Skill UP!* Then play a game in groups of four. Use the *Key phrases* to help you.

Skill UP! When you are playing a game or doing an activity with friends and need to stop the other players so that you can ask, explain or check something, you can say:
Wait a minute.
Hang on a second.
Can I just ask / say / check … ?
Use a pleasant tone of voice to be polite.

- Use the table below for your group.

Heads	last year	a hero	health and fitness	an outdoor event
Tails	next year	parks	art and design	good deeds

- Take turns to play.
- Throw a coin to decide which row of topics to choose from, heads or tails.
- Choose one of the topics and talk about it for 20 seconds without stopping.
- If you succeed, score one point and cross out the topic.
- If you fail, all the other players score one point. Don't cross out the topic. Another player can choose it.
- The game ends when all the topics are crossed out. The person with the most points is the winner.

5.6 #CHECK THIS OUT!

LESSON OBJECTIVES • Write an online advert • Learn style tips for writing online adverts

WRITING

1 💬 Do you agree or disagree with these opinions about online advertising? Why?
  1 I like seeing adverts for products and events that interest me.
  2 I find online adverts really annoying.

2 Read online adverts 1 and 2. Answer the questions.
  1 What can people do at Astro Park Funfair?
  2 What is inside the Abracadabra Magic Set?

1 ASTRO PARK FUNFAIR

Astro Park Funfair We're the place to be this summer! You finally finished school and now you're free!!! Bring your friends to Astro Park. Enjoy the exciting funfair rides, visit our amazing souvenir stalls or get something to eat at one of our delicious food trucks. There's nowhere as good as Astro Park! For groups of four or more, one person gets in free!

2 Abracadabra — Own the magic

Do you dream of being a great magician? Would you like to surprise your friends with incredible tricks? The Abracadabra Magic Set is now available worldwide. There are over 20 great tricks in the box, plus video instructions on how to perform them. You will love this high-quality beginner's magic set, so ORDER YOURS TODAY. (Rabbit not included.)
#ownthemagic #abracadabra

3 💬 **MEDIATION** Which online advert do you think is the most effective and why? Tell your classmates in English.

4 Read adverts 1 and 2 again. Answer the questions.
  1 Which advert uses:
     • exclamation marks (!)? _____
     • CAPITAL LETTERS? _____
  2 Which advert includes a video? _____
  3 Which advert includes questions? _____
  4 Which advert uses hashtags (#)? _____

5 Read the *Skill UP!* Then complete it with the headings in the box.

Audience   Formality   Hashtags(#)   Length   Visuals

Skill UP!
Writing an online advert
Follow these tips:
1 _____: Short (50–100 words) is usually good for online adverts.
2 _____: Try to include a photo with your advert.
3 _____: Use informal language, exclamation marks (!) and CAPITAL LETTERS.
4 _____: Talk directly to the people who will read your advert. Ask them questions.
5 _____: Use these to connect your advert to a larger discussion.

PROJECT BUILDER 5
Write an online advert for a games club.

➡ Workbook **Project Log** p22

6 Write an online advert for the school website about a games club where students can play with your set of games and challenges as well as other games. Work in groups for Part A only.

A Plan
  • What is the name of the games club?
  • Where is the club? When is it open?
  • What is your set of games and challenges called?

B Write
  • Follow the tips in the *Skill UP!* and write your advert.

C Read and check
  • Check that your advert has an informal style.
  • Check your spelling and grammar.

65

5 PROJECT

Make a set of games and challenges

SHARE AND REVIEW

Use your Project Log → p20–22

1. Look back at your Project Builders 1–5 for this unit. In which Project Builder did you:
   - **A** write a set of fun challenges? 2
   - **B** write an online advert? ....
   - **C** prepare a revision word game? ....
   - **D** create a wordsearch puzzle? ....
   - **E** create a memory game with a paragraph and a grid? ....

2. Share and review the work from your Project Builders. Is there anything you want to change?

DECIDE

3. Read the tasks for creating your set of games and challenges. Choose roles for each member of your group. More than one person can work on the same task.

Project planner	Front of card	Back of card	
Project tasks	quiz games	games where people answer questions to test their knowledge and memory	Who?
REVISION WORD GAME Project Builder 1 Write each of the words from your group on the front of a card or small piece of paper. Write the definition on the back. Put all the cards together to make a set.			
CHALLENGES Project Builder 2 Create a page for your five challenges. Add pictures of the challenges, where helpful, and make it look attractive.			
MEMORY GAME Project Builder 3 Create a page for your memory game. Include your paragraph and the picture grid. Add instructions for the game to the page.			
WORDSEARCH PUZZLES Project Builder 4 Create a page for your wordsearch puzzles. Include all the wordsearch puzzles from your group. Write the answers on the back of the page.			
FOLDER Project Builder 5 Create a folder for your set of games and challenges. Write the name of the set on the front of the folder and add pictures or drawings to make it look attractive. Put a copy of one of your adverts for a games club inside the folder for players to read.			

66

CREATE

4 Complete the instructions for the word game from Project Builder 1. Use the words in the box.

| guess   play   put   don't show   take   use |

5 Read the *Project skills*. Then write instructions for the memory game from Project Builder 3. Use the words in the box.

PROJECT SKILLS — Writing instructions
- Organize the instructions as bullet points instead of one long text.
- Write clear instructions that are easy to follow.
- Use simple language, for example:
  Take a card.   Don't write on it.   Read the word to the group.
- Ask another person to read your instructions and check they are clear.

| cover   groups   paragraph   picture grid   play   read
remember   say   two minutes |

6 Create your set of games and challenges. Complete the rest of the tasks from the project planner in exercise 3.

Instructions for our word game
- ¹_____ as two teams.
- First, ²_____ all the cards in one pile with the words down and the definitions up.
- Team A: ³_____ the top card and read out the definition. ⁴_____ team B the word.
- Team B: ⁵_____ the word.
- Correct answer = 1 point
  Wrong answer = 0 points
- Take turns (A, B, A, B).
- ⁶_____ all the cards.
- The team with the most points wins!

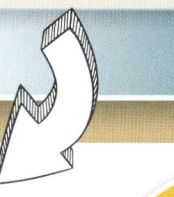

PLAY

7 Swap your set of games and challenges with another group and complete the activities. Then discuss the questions as a group.
1 Which were your favourite activities?
2 Which activities were the most difficult?
3 How successful were you at the activities?
4 Can you think of any ways to improve the other group's project?

8 Use your answers to exercise 7 to give some feedback to the other group.

PROJECT COACH ▶ Video

REFLECT

9 Think about your project work in this unit. Read the statements and choose your reaction.

COLLABORATION
1 I can work with others to discuss and give feedback.
☹ 😐 🙂 😊 😁

CREATIVITY
2 Our group can create activities that are not too easy and not too difficult.
☹ 😐 🙂 😊 😁

COMMUNICATION
3 Our group can write clear instructions.
☹ 😐 🙂 😊 😁

10 Complete these sentences for you.
1 I am pleased with our set of games and challenges because _____
2 I want to improve _____

➔ Workbook **Project Log** p23

67

6 Move it!

UNIT OBJECTIVES

YOUR PROJECT Create a health and fitness infographic

Project Builders 1–5:
1. Prepare the *Healthy mornings* section of your infographic.
2. Prepare the *Fitness* section.
3. Prepare the *Healthy eating* section.
4. Prepare the *Personal hygiene* section.
5. Write a survey report.

Display your infographic.

VOCABULARY
- Exercise and the body
- Personal hygiene

GRAMMAR
- Present perfect
- Present perfect with *ever* and *never*

Start your day the healthy way ... with breakfast!

Research shows that about 25% of teenagers in the USA don't eat breakfast.

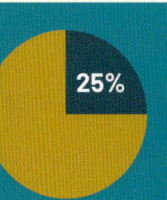

25%

Why is breakfast good?

Studies show links between:

1 eating breakfast and doing better at school.

2 eating breakfast and doing better at sports and exercise.

Eat a healthy breakfast every day. It's good for you!

LESSON OBJECTIVES • Talk about morning routines • Learn vocabulary for talking about morning routines

WARM-UP

1. 💬 **Look at the infographic and discuss the questions.**
   1. Why is it a good idea to eat breakfast?
   2. Give an example of a healthy breakfast.

2. 💬 **MEDIATION** A friend doesn't speak English. With your partner, explain the infographic on page 68 to them in your own language.

3. ▶ Video **Watch Curtis and Amanda's vlog. Who has items 1–7 for breakfast? Label them Curtis (C) or Amanda (A). Who has the healthiest breakfast?**
1	C	Banana	4	___	Orange juice	6	___	Tea
2	___	Brown bread	5	___	Spinach	7	___	Water
3	___	Eggs						

4. ▶ Video **Watch again and answer the questions.**
   1. In what other ways is Curtis's morning different to Amanda's?
   2. Whose Saturday morning is most similar to yours?

Curtis and Amanda's VLOG
Good morning?
07:00

5. **Complete the questions with the words in the box.**

   | alarm   asleep   energy   fit   fresh   get up |
   | lifestyle   personal hygiene   wake up |

   1. Do you use an _____ to help you wake up in the morning?
   2. Do you usually _____ soon after you _____ or do you like to stay in bed for a while?
   3. Do you usually feel _____ and full of _____ after you get out of bed or tired and still half _____?
   4. Do you do your _____ routine (e.g. brush your teeth and wash) before or after breakfast?
   5. Do you think exercising in the morning is an important part of a _____ and healthy _____?

6. 💬 **Discuss the questions in exercise 5. Which of you is more of a 'morning person'?**

7. 💬 **THINK** How could you make your mornings healthier? Discuss.

PROJECT BUILDER 1   Prepare the *Healthy mornings* section of your infographic.

→ **Workbook Project Log** p24

8. 👥 Your project is to create a health and fitness infographic. Your infographic will have four sections. Prepare the text for the *Healthy mornings* section. Write five pieces of advice for a healthy morning.

   It is good to get eight hours of sleep before you get up in the morning.

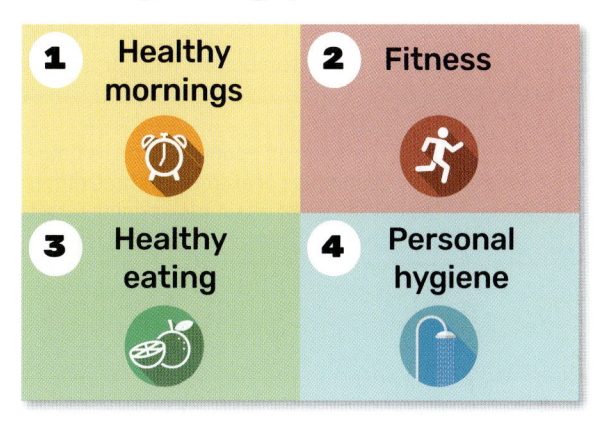

   | 1 Healthy mornings | 2 Fitness |
   | 3 Healthy eating | 4 Personal hygiene |

6.2 FITNESS FAQs

LESSON OBJECTIVES • Understand the importance of exercise for teenagers • Learn vocabulary related to exercise and the body • Use the present perfect to talk about experiences

VOCABULARY

1 💬 Discuss the questions.
1 How is exercise good for you?
2 How much exercise do teenagers need to do?
3 Is it possible to do too much exercise?
4 What's the best kind of exercise to do?

2 Read Anya's blog and complete gaps A–D with questions 1–4 from exercise 1.

Anya-keeps-fit!
teenage fitness

Home Blog Top Tips FAQs

A _____ It's best to exercise in a variety of ways if you want to get fit. Try aerobic exercise for your heart and lungs, strength training to build your muscles and stretching to keep them flexible.

B _____ Keeping fit is good for your brain and your body. Exercising produces chemicals (called endorphins) that make you happy. Regular training helps you sleep better, and reduces your risk of illness. It also helps you burn calories, lose weight and even keeps your bones strong.

C _____ Experts recommend 60 minutes per day for teenagers. Warm up before you train and stretch when you have finished. I usually rest one day a week.

D _____ Teenage bodies need calories to develop. Using all your energy for exercise can slow your physical development. Do the recommended amount of regular exercise correctly and safely. If you feel any pain, stop before you get an injury.

LIFE SKILLS Try to do an hour of exercise a day. This could be 20 minutes of exercise at three different times of the day. It can be as simple as going for a fast walk. When is the best time for you to exercise?

3 Match the highlighted words in Anya's blog to the categories.
1 actions related to exercise (×7)
....
2 parts of the body (×5)
....
3 the effects of unsafe exercise (×2)
....

4 Match words 1–3 from Anya's blog with the pictures A–C.
1 aerobic exercise 2 strength training 3 stretching

5 Read the live chat from Anya's blog. Answer the questions.
1 What is Anya's favourite type of exercise?
2 What type of exercise does Anya recommend for Sergio?

Live chat

Josh What's your favourite type of exercise, Anya?

Anya I've done lots of different types of exercise. My favourite is CrossFit. I love doing strength training with other people. Have you tried CrossFit, Josh?

Josh No, I haven't. It looks great though. I'll try it. Thanks!

Clara My friend Sergio wants to exercise with his dog. He's tried jogging, but his dog didn't like it! Can you suggest anything?

Anya Have you heard of Doga? There has been a lot about it online recently. It's like yoga, but you do it with your dog! 📎

Clara Wow, cute! No, I haven't heard of this before. I'm sure my friend hasn't either. Thanks, Anya.

6 MEDIATION Look online and find out more about CrossFit for teenagers or Doga. Tell a classmate two interesting things about either of these activities in English.

GRAMMAR
Present perfect

7 Study the language from the live chat in exercise 5. Then complete the table.

Affirmative and negative			
Subject		have	Past participle
+	I / You / We / They	have / 've	⁴ _____ lots of different types of exercise.
−		have not / ¹ _____	
+	He / She / It	has / ² _____	⁵ _____ jogging.
−		has not / ³ _____	
Questions			Short answers
⁶ _____ you tried CrossFit?			Yes, I have. / No, I ⁷ _____ .
Has he tried CrossFit?			Yes, he has. / No, he hasn't.

We use the present perfect when we ⁸ **want** / **don't want** to mention a specific time in the past.

We say *there is* and *there are* in the present perfect using ⁹ _____ and ¹⁰ _____ .

CHECK IT! ➡ MY GRAMMAR REFERENCE & PRACTICE p116

8 Complete the sentences with the present perfect form of the words in brackets.
1 We _____ (try) Zumba.
2 I _____ (not do) strength training.
3 Tim _____ (learn) how to stretch safely.
4 _____ (you run) 10 km?
5 Rachael _____ (not use) a fitness app.

9 Write sentences in the present perfect using the prompts below and the live chat in exercise 5.

Anya / do lots of different types of exercise.
Anya has done lots of different types of exercise.
1 Josh / try CrossFit.
2 Sergio / try jogging with his dog.
3 Clara / heard of Doga before.
4 Sergio and his dog / join a Doga class.

10 🔊 **24** Read the *Pronunciation*, then listen. Can you hear the strong and weak forms of *have* and *has*? Listen again and repeat.

PRONUNCIATION Strong and weak forms of *have* and *has*		
	Strong form	Weak form
have	/hæv/	/həv/
has	/hæz/	/həz/

11 Complete the live chat post with the present perfect affirmative form of the verbs in brackets.

Leo Hi Anya. I started exercising regularly when I was 13. I wasn't fit then, but I am now! There ¹ _____ (be) good times and difficult times on my fitness journey. I ² _____ (make) some brilliant friends and we ³ _____ (share) the pleasure and the pain of getting fit! I'm very proud of some of my achievements. For example, I ⁴ _____ (run) a 5 km race and I ⁵ _____ (learn) how to lift weights safely. I ⁶ _____ (write) a blog about my experiences, and there ⁷ _____ (be) a really positive response. I ⁸ _____ (enjoy) your blog a lot, Anya. Getting fit has changed my life!

12 💬 Use *have* and *haven't* to talk about the ideas in the box. Ask each other questions.

| do strength training   exercise at an outdoor gym |
| feel muscle pain after exercise   go to an exercise class |
| have a sports injury   play sports in a team   run 5 km |
| swim 1 km   try yoga (or Doga!)   use a fitness app |

> I've tried yoga.   Where did you do it?

PROJECT BUILDER 2

Prepare the *Fitness* section of your infographic.

➡ Workbook **Project Log** p24

13 👥 Read the text. Can you think of any other benefits of playing roller hockey?

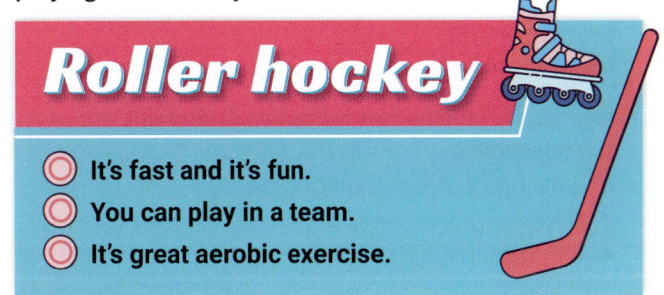

Roller hockey
○ It's fast and it's fun.
○ You can play in a team.
○ It's great aerobic exercise.

14 👥 Discuss to find three types of sport or exercise that you have all tried and enjoyed.

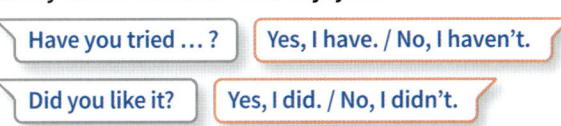

> Have you tried … ?   Yes, I have. / No, I haven't.
> Did you like it?   Yes, I did. / No, I didn't.

15 👥 Prepare the text for the *Fitness* section of your infographic. Write three benefits for each of the types of sport or exercise that you chose in exercise 14.

6.3 JUNK FOOD

LESSON OBJECTIVES
- Learn about junk food
- Use cognates while reading
- Use the present perfect with *ever* and *never*

Dump the junk!

It's not easy to cut down on junk food. We know it's bad for us, but it tastes great, feels good in our mouths and comes in so many varieties. Here are some healthier ways to enjoy the things we love about junk food.

Strong flavours

The strong flavours of salt, sugar, and fat make us want to keep on eating junk food, even when we know we should stop. We really only need small amounts of salt, fat and sugar as part of a healthy diet.

Look for strong flavours in healthy foods – spicy pepper or chili, sharp vinegar or lemon, and sweet fresh fruit. Healthy foods taste good, too.

Interesting textures

Food companies design junk food to feel good in our mouths. We really enjoy snacks that are crunchy outside with a soft middle full of flavour.

Remember, you'll also come across interesting textures in healthy food: crunchy raw carrots or nuts, soft tasty hummus or avocado, chewy dried fruit, and grapes that explode in your mouth!

Lots of variety

Food companies come up with a wide variety of flavours, colours, shapes and sizes for their products. Just look at breakfast cereal! Your brain easily gets bored, so it loves variety.

You don't have to give up junk food completely. Balance it with healthy food of all different flavours, colours and textures. Healthy food doesn't have to be boring!

READING

1 Look at the photos in the article and discuss the questions.
  1. What types of junk food can you see?
  2. Which do you eat regularly? Which do you never eat?
  3. Why do you think people like junk food so much?

2 Read the *Skill UP!* then scan the article 'Dump the junk!' Are there any cognates? Underline similarities in the spelling. What differences in pronunciation are there?

> **Skill UP!**
> **Use your own language to understand English**
> Some English words sound or look similar in other languages. When the meaning is the same in both languages, these words are called 'cognates'. Scan texts quickly for cognates and use them to help you work out the topic.

3 🔊 25 Read and listen to the article. Check your ideas from exercise 1 question 3.

4 **MEDIATION** Imagine you are talking to a young child. With your partner, explain in your own language why too much junk food is bad. Give three reasons.

5 Are the statements about the article true (T) or false (F)?
  1. It explains why people like eating junk food. ____
  2. It describes the effects of eating too much junk food. ____
  3. It explains how to cook healthier junk food at home. ____
  4. It suggests healthy alternatives to junk food. ____
  5. It tells readers to stop eating junk food completely. ____
  6. It recommends a balanced diet. ____

6 Match the highlighted phrasal verbs in the article to definitions 1–6 below.
  1. try to find ____
  2. continue doing something ____
  3. stop doing, or having, something ____
  4. suggest, invent, or think of something ____
  5. eat or do less of something ____
  6. find something by chance ____

GRAMMAR

Present perfect with *ever* and *never*

7 🔊 26 Listen to Kirsten and Magnus trying some healthy food. Answer the questions.
1 What food do they try?
....
....
2 What do they think of the food?
....
....

8 Study sentences A and B from Kirsten and Magnus's conversation. Then choose the correct option to complete the rules.
A I've never tried banana chips.
B Have you ever eaten popcorn?

Present perfect with *ever* and *never*

We use the present perfect with *ever* and *never* to talk about life experience up to now.
- ¹ **Ever** / **Never** means 'at any time in the past' and ² **ever** / **never** means 'at no time in the past'.
- We use *never* + a(n) ³ **affirmative** / **negative** verb form to talk about experiences you or other people didn't have.
- We usually use ⁴ **ever** / **never** in questions and ⁵ **ever** / **never** in answers.

CHECK IT! ➡ MY GRAMMAR REFERENCE & PRACTICE p116

✅ *Kirsten and Magnus have **been** to a health-food shop.*
= They went, then came back.
*Kirsten and Magnus have **gone** to a health-food shop.*
= They are still at the health food shop.

---

9 Complete the sentences with *ever* or *never*.
1 Has Cleo .... tried to give up junk food?
2 I've .... eaten junk food for breakfast.
3 Have you .... kept on eating junk food even though you were full?
4 I've .... looked for a healthy option in a fast-food restaurant.
5 Has Paul .... been to a health food shop?
6 We've .... made French fries at home.

10 Complete the mini dialogues using the present perfect and the words in brackets. Add *ever* or *never* where possible.
1 A <u>Have you ever had</u> (you have) banana chips, Maddie?
  B No, ..., but .... (try) garlic popcorn.
2 A Where's Araf?
  B He .... (go) to Big Burger for lunch.
  A Oh, I .... (not go) there. Have you?
  B No, I haven't. I .... (go) to Burger Boy, but not Big Burger. Shall we try it one day?
3 A .... (you order) chocolate pizza, Keyla?
  B Yes, ... It was far too sweet.

11 Write sentences that are true for you. Use *never* and the present perfect form of the verbs in the box.

| eat | drink | go | meet | play / do |
| read | see | try | | |

1 an unhealthy food
  I've never tried chocolate pizza.
2 a healthy food
3 a drink
4 a famous film
5 a type of sport or exercise
6 a city or country
7 a celebrity
8 a famous book

12 💬 Make questions with *ever* using your answers from exercise 11. Then ask and answer.

> Have you ever tried chocolate pizza?

> Yes, I have! It was delicious!

PROJECT BUILDER 3

Prepare the *Healthy eating* section of your infographic.

➡ Workbook **Project Log** p25

13 👥 Ask and answer present perfect questions about 1–6 below.
1 think about how much junk food you eat
2 try to give up junk food
3 look for healthy snacks instead of crisps or chocolate
4 choose vegetarian burgers or sausages instead of meat ones
5 eat crunchy vegetables as a snack
6 drink water instead of sugary drinks

> Have you ever thought about how much junk food you eat?

14 👥 Write three pieces of advice about food and drink to include in the *Healthy eating* section of your infographic. Use ideas from exercise 13 or your own.

Try to give up junk food. If you can't give it up completely, try to avoid eating it more than once a week. It's bad for your health.

6.4 HYGIENE

LESSON OBJECTIVES
- Listen to an expert talk about personal hygiene
- Learn personal hygiene collocations
- Listen for detail

LISTENING

1 What personal hygiene tips do you know?

> You should wash your hands before eating.

> And shower regularly. What else?

2 Complete the quiz.

How much do you know about personal hygiene?

1. How often should you shower?
2. How long does it take to brush your teeth properly?
3. How often do experts say you need to visit the dentist?
4. Can your phone give you spots?
5. Sweat smells. True or False?
6. What is the difference between a deodorant and an antiperspirant?
7. Should you use your hand to cover your mouth when you cough or sneeze?
8. How long does it take to wash your hands properly?

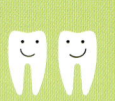

3 Read the *Skill UP!* Which quiz questions are asking about a length of time?

Skill UP! Before you listen for answers to questions, study the questions and think about what kind of detail you need to listen for. For example:
- A question with *How long* could be asking for a 'length of time', e.g. *one hour*.
- A question with *How often* is asking about frequency, or a 'number of times', e.g. *six times a day*, *every year*.

4 🔊 27 Listen to a hygiene expert and check your answers to the quiz.

74

VOCABULARY

5 Match the verbs in the box to a group of words 1–6 to make collocations.

| brush   change   cut   go   prevent   use |

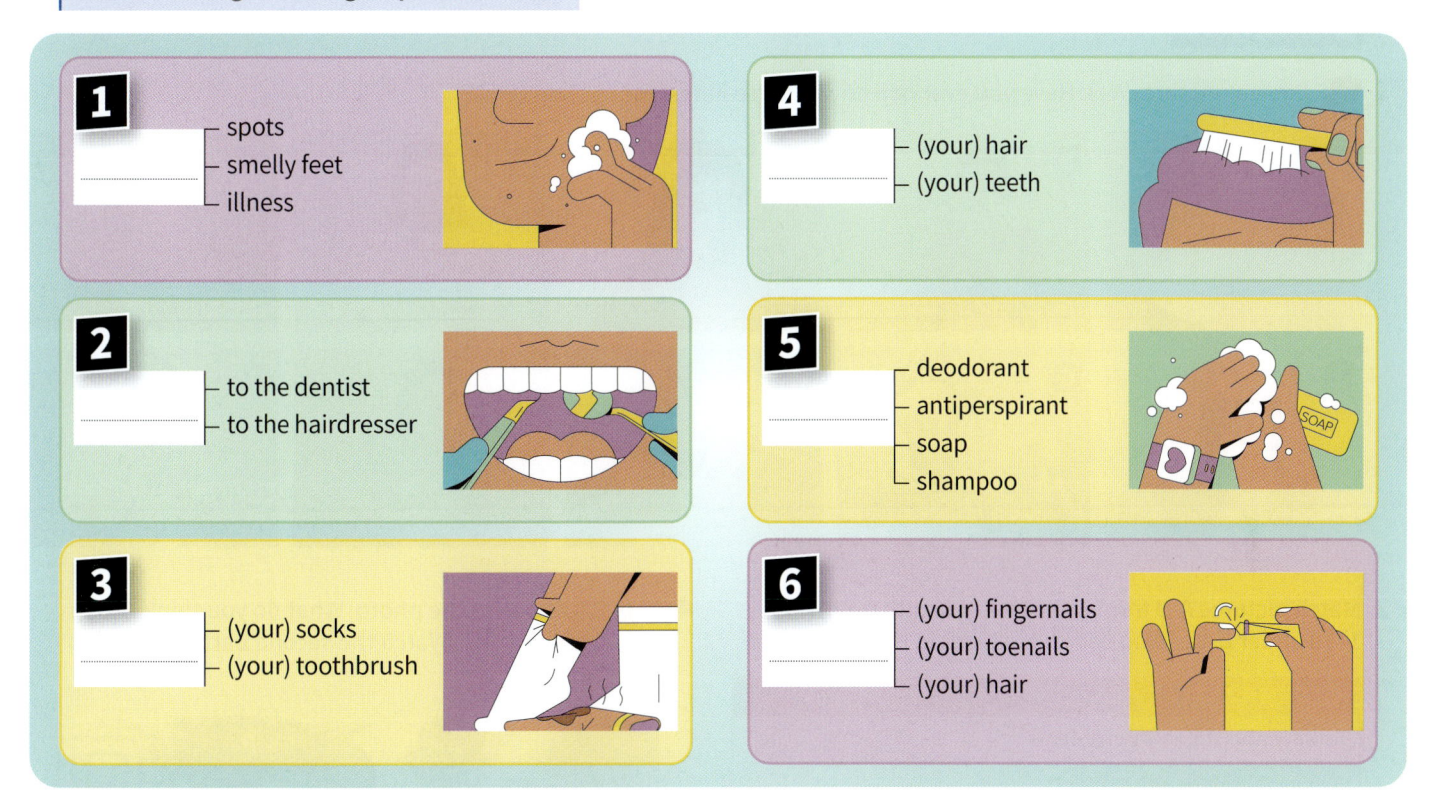

1 ____
- spots
- smelly feet
- illness

2 ____
- to the dentist
- to the hairdresser

3 ____
- (your) socks
- (your) toothbrush

4 ____
- (your) hair
- (your) teeth

5 ____
- deodorant
- antiperspirant
- soap
- shampoo

6 ____
- (your) fingernails
- (your) toenails
- (your) hair

6 Complete the sentences with collocations from exercise 5.
1. _____ to reduce the amount you sweat.
2. Change your socks every day to help _____ .
3. Every time I _____ , I fall asleep while she is cutting my hair.
4. I forgot my toothbrush so I had to _____ with my finger.
5. Grandad didn't _____ and they made holes in his socks!
6. The dentist told me I should _____ every three months.

7 💬 Ask and answer questions about the collocations in exercise 5. Use the question prompts below.
- How can you … ?
- When do you … ?
- How often do / should you … ?
- Why do people use … ?

> How can you prevent smelly feet?

> It helps to change your socks regularly.

PROJECT BUILDER 4
Prepare the *Personal hygiene* section of your infographic.

➡ Workbook **Project Log** p25

8 👥 Agree on the five most important personal hygiene tips.

9 👥 Prepare the text for the *Fitness* section of your infographic. Write down your top five tips from exercise 8. Give a reason for each tip.

It is very important to wash your hands regularly. You should do this after you go to the toilet and before you eat or prepare food. This can help prevent illness.

6.5 WHAT'S THE MATTER?

LESSON OBJECTIVES • Talk about health problems • Learn how to express sympathy

SPEAKING

1 💬 Look at pictures A–J. Have you ever had any of these illnesses?

2 Match pictures A–J from exercise 1 to health problems 1–10 under *Describing health problems* in the *Key phrases*.

KEY PHRASES
Talking about health problems

Asking about health problems

¹ .... you all right?
What's ² .... matter?
Where does it hurt?
Does your head ³ .... ?
Have you ⁴ .... a temperature?
How do you feel?

Describing health problems

1 ...... I feel (awful / terrible / ill).
2 ...... I feel sick.
3 ...... I've got a temperature.
4 ...... My back hurts. / I've hurt my back.
5 ...... I've got a sore throat.
6 ...... I've got stomach ache.
7 ...... I've got toothache.
8 ...... I've got a cough.
9 ...... I've got a headache.
10 ...... I've got a cold.

3 ▶Video Watch the first part of the video. Complete the *Key phrases*. Which phrases does Amy use to describe her health problems?

4 ▶Video Look at the photo. What do you think happened to Lucy? Watch the second part of the video and check.

5 💬 Read the *Skill UP!* Then choose one of the situations below or use your own idea. Take turns asking what happened and how your partner feels. Express sympathy and offer some advice.

Skill UP! When someone tells you they don't feel well, you can express sympathy with one of these phrases. Use a sad tone of voice.
Oh dear. Oh no! Poor you. You poor thing.

- You have a bad cold.
- You were looking at your phone and walked into a door.
- You fell off your chair in class.
- You broke your tooth eating something hard.

6.6 WRITING A REPORT

LESSON OBJECTIVES • Write a survey report • Learn how to organize information in a report

WRITING

1 Read and complete the report. Match questions 1–3 with gaps A–C.
1 What do you do to relax?
2 Have you ever worried about school?
3 What else do you worry about?

> This report shows the results of our class survey. We asked ten students what they worry about, and what they do to relax. The results are quite surprising.
> **A** ____ Most students have worried about school. Only two people have never worried about school.
> **B** ____ More than half the students worry about their appearance. A few feel stressed about the environment. None of the people in our survey worry about their future jobs.
> **C** ____ All the students we asked spend time with friends when they want to relax. Half play video games with their friends and some watch TV together.
> In conclusion, the survey shows that our classmates worry about similar things and relax in similar ways.

2 Read the report again and answer the questions. Then read the *Skill UP!* and check.
1 How many paragraphs are there in the report?
2 Which paragraph(s):
  • report the results of the survey questions?
  • summarize the results of the survey?
  • explain what the survey was about?

Skill UP! Writing a survey report
1 Paragraph 1: Tell the reader what your survey was about and how many people you asked. Make a general comment about the results.
2 Paragraphs 2, 3 and 4: Report the results of the survey questions.
3 Paragraph 5: Give a conclusion. Say what the results of the survey show.

3 Study the highlighted quantifiers in the report. Add them to the line below. Two of the quantifiers have a similar meaning. Put these in the same place.

LARGEST quantity ———————————— SMALLEST quantity

4 Complete each sentence with a quantifier from exercise 3. Use the information in brackets (5/10 = 5 out of the 10 people in the survey).
1 _____ of the people have never been to a gym. (5/10)
2 _____ of our classmates like eating burgers. (9/10)
3 _____ of the students go to bed before 10 p.m. (0/10)
4 _____ of the people in the survey enjoy team sports. (6/10)
5 _____ pupils have stayed awake for 24 hours. (3/10)
6 _____ of the people we asked brush their teeth twice a day, every day. (10/10)

PROJECT BUILDER 5

Write a survey report.

→ Workbook **Project Log** p26

5 Prepare a class survey on a health and fitness topic and write a report about it. Work in groups for Part A only.

A Write and do your class survey
• Choose one of the topics from your infographic and write three questions for your survey, each with two to four possible answers. Use *Have you ever … ?* for one of your questions.

healthy mornings   fitness   healthy eating personal hygiene

Question 1: Have you ever worried about school?
A yes
B no

• Ask your questions to 8–10 classmates and record the results.
Results:
A: ✓✓✓✓✓✓✓✓ (8 students)
B: ✓✓ (2 students)

B Write your report
• Follow the tips in the *Skill UP!* and write a report about the results of your survey.
• Use quantifiers.

C Read and check
• Check your report has five paragraphs.
• Check you have used appropriate quantifiers.

77

6 PROJECT

Create a health and fitness infographic

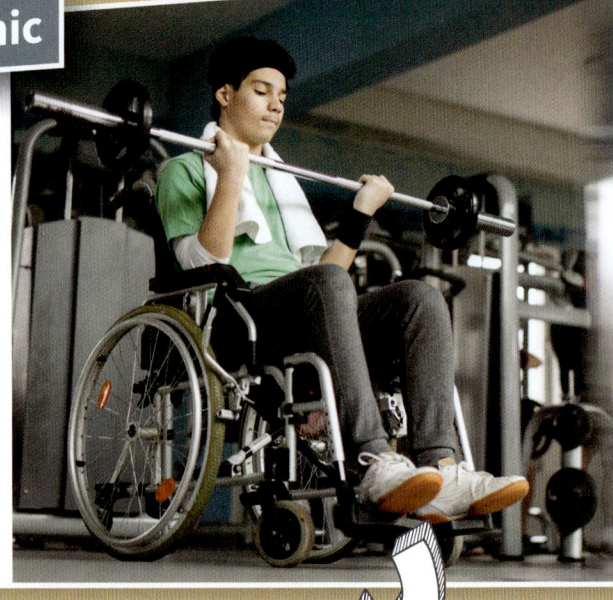

SHARE AND REVIEW

Use your Project Log → p24–26

1. 👥 Look back at your Project Builders 1–5 for this unit. Which Project Builder is about:
   - **A** personal hygiene? 4
   - **B** fitness? ......
   - **C** healthy eating? ......
   - **D** a survey report? ......
   - **E** healthy mornings? ......

2. 👥 Share and review the work from your Project Builders. Is there anything you want to change?

ANALYSE

What is an infographic?

An infographic is a visual way to show information and data quickly and clearly.

Did you know?

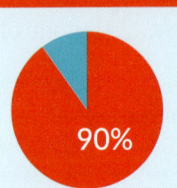

90% of the information processed by your brain is visual.

The brain processes visual information 60,000 times faster than text.

Different ways to show data

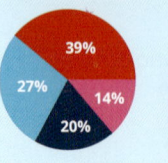

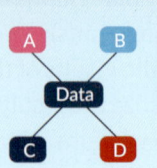

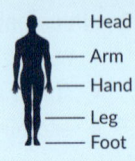

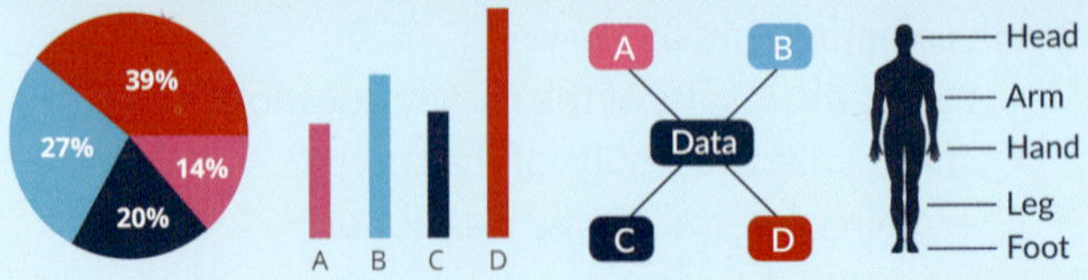

pie chart | bar chart | mind map | diagram

What makes a great infographic?

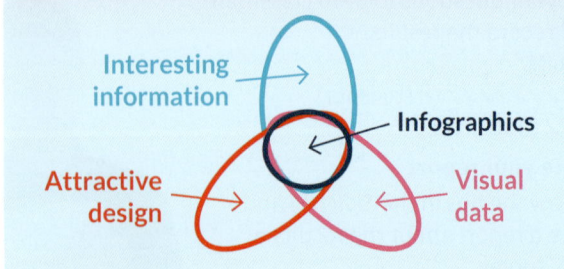

Interesting information · Attractive design · Visual data → Infographics

Have you ever made an infographic?

Here are three important tips:

Tip 1: Use no more than five colours.
Tip 2: Use the same or similar fonts for all your text.
Tip 3: Use headings and sub-headings to make the information clear.

3. Find the following features in the infographic above.
   1. information as text
   2. numbers
   3. tips
   4. headings and sub-headings
   5. visual data, e.g. charts or diagrams
   6. a question in the present perfect with *ever*

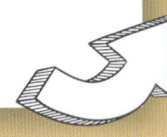

78

CREATE

4 Read the *Project skills*. Can you think of any other tips for dealing with disagreements during project work?

PROJECT SKILLS Dealing with disagreements
- Stay calm. Don't shout or get angry.
- Listen to everyone's opinions and work together to find solutions.
- Be kind and fair. Try to find fair solutions, e.g. 'If we use your idea here, can we use my idea there?'

5 Create your infographic on a large piece of paper. Follow steps 1–6 below. Try to deal with any disagreements while you work.

1. Divide the page into four sections. Use one section for each Project Builder 1–4.
2. Try to include all of your written work (your advice and tips etc.) from Project Builders 1–4 in your infographic.
3. Include the results of your survey from Project Builder 5 by creating charts or diagrams from the data and adding them to your infographic.
4. Design your infographic using the tips from page 78. It is also a good idea to look at examples of infographics online.
5. Display your finished infographic on a classroom wall or table for the other students to read.
6. Leave a blank piece of paper next to your infographic for feedback from other students.

PROJECT COACH ▶ Video

REACT

6 Walk around the classroom and read the other groups' infographics. React to any interesting information in them. Use the *Key phrases* to help.

KEY PHRASES
Reacting to information
- That's interesting!
- I didn't know that (swimming was so good for you).
- I'm surprised that (only two students like junk food).
- I've read / heard / seen something about that before.

7 Write feedback for each group on the blank piece of paper next to their infographic. Comment on the following points.
- one thing you liked
- one thing that surprised you
- one suggestion for improving the infographic

8 Go back to your infographic and read the feedback. Which is the most helpful comment?

REFLECT

9 Think about your project work in this unit. Read the statements and choose your reaction.

COLLABORATION
1 Our group can deal with disagreements.
☹ 😐 🙂 😊 🤩

CREATIVITY
2 Our group can present visual information in different ways.
☹ 😐 🙂 😊 🤩

COMMUNICATION
3 Our group can talk about experiences.
☹ 😐 🙂 😊 🤩

10 Complete these sentences for you.
1 I am pleased with our infographic because _____
2 I want to improve _____

➡ Workbook **Project Log** p27

7 Skills for life

UNIT OBJECTIVES

YOUR PROJECT Create a how-to video

Project Builders 1–5:
1. Make a list of possible topics.
2. Choose your final topic and write some instructions.
3. Prepare and plan.
4. Share tips and skills with your classmates.
5. Write the final instructions and cue cards.

Present your how-to video.

VOCABULARY
- Verbs and their noun forms
- Verbs

GRAMMAR
- should / shouldn't, must / mustn't
- have (got) to + infinitive without to

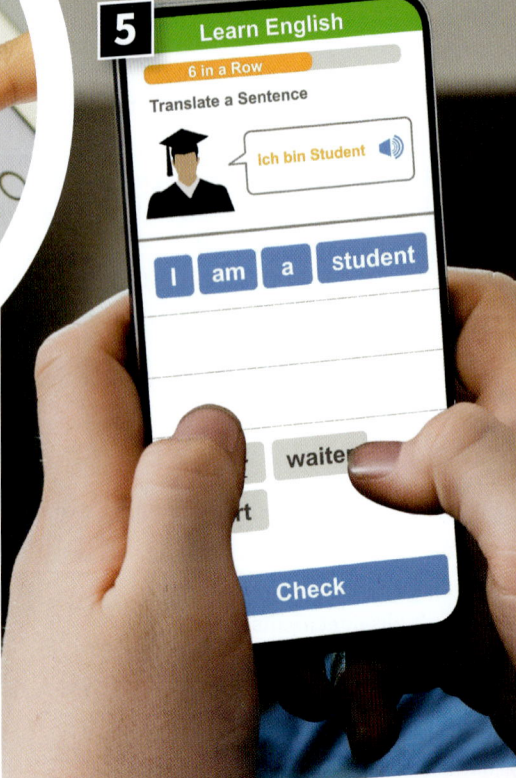

LESSON OBJECTIVES • Talk about online learning • Learn vocabulary related to online learning

WARM-UP

1. **Look at photos 1–5. Discuss the questions.**
   1. What kind of learning do the photos show?
   2. What equipment for learning can you see in the photos?

2. ▶ Video **Watch Curtis and Amanda's vlog. Answer the questions.**
   1. What are Curtis, Amanda and Sarah making for their school project?
   2. What examples of how-to videos do they mention? Name four.

3. **How many tips for learning with the internet can you remember from the vlog?**

4. ▶ Video **Complete the sentences from the video with the words in the box. Then watch again and check.**

answers   distract   engine   fact   find   focused   learn   resources   search   subject

   1. The internet is … a brilliant place to _____ from others and find _____ to your questions.
   2. Let's look at how to use online _____ to help you learn.
   3. Ask your parents, teachers, or classmates about good websites, blogs and vlogs where you can _____ for information or research a _____.
   4. Websites with .gov or .edu in their addresses are usually reliable places to _____ out about something or check a _____.
   5. Use a search _____ you know well.
   6. How can I stay _____ while learning online?
   7. Advertisements and links can easily _____ you from what you are doing.

5. **Discuss the questions.**
   1. What search engine do you usually use?
   2. How do you check facts that you find online?
   3. Do you find it hard to stay focused when you are learning online? Why / Why not?

PROJECT BUILDER 1   Make a list of possible topics.

→ **Workbook Project Log** p28

6. **Look at the titles for how-to videos on the right. Which video do you think was:**
   1. the easiest to make?
   2. the most difficult to make?
   3. the most fun to make?

7. **Read the tips below, then make a list of four possible topics for your how-to video.**
   • Try to think of your own ideas.
   • Choose topics that you already know a lot about.
   • Choose topics that are easy to film.
   • Choose topics that you can explain in less than five minutes.

Curtis and Amanda's VLOG
How to learn with the internet

How to make bread
How to make a music video on your phone
How to eat with CHOPSTICKS
How to draw a person

7.2 YOUR SKILFUL BRAIN

LESSON OBJECTIVES
- Learn about the brain
- Learn verbs and their noun forms
- Use *should / shouldn't* and *must / mustn't* to talk about advice, obligation and prohibition

VOCABULARY

1 💬 Look at the diagram. Say what the different parts of your brain do.

> The front of your brain controls behaviour, personality, movement and memory.

> The top of your brain controls …

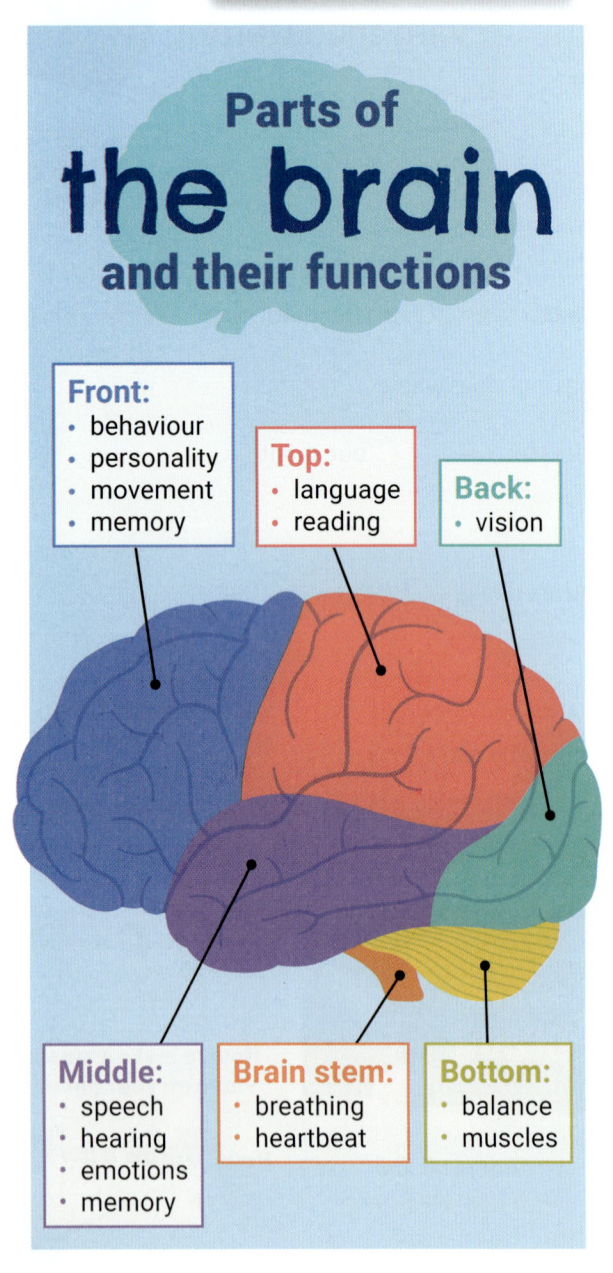

Parts of the brain and their functions

Front:
- behaviour
- personality
- movement
- memory

Top:
- language
- reading

Back:
- vision

Middle:
- speech
- hearing
- emotions
- memory

Brain stem:
- breathing
- heartbeat

Bottom:
- balance
- muscles

2 Read about a podcast. Who is it for? What will listeners learn?

Your Skilful Brain 🎙 Podcast

Your skilful brain is responsible for every feeling you have, every decision you make and every goal you achieve. It can respond quickly when there is a problem and is brilliant at finding a solution. Your brain stores huge amounts of knowledge, but can also remember small details.

This week's podcast is especially for teenagers (and their brains). We talk to brain expert Liang Zhao about how to look after your growing brain and train it to make learning easier.

Click here to listen

3 Complete the table with words from the diagram in exercise 1 and the text in exercise 2.

Verb	Noun
	achievement
behave	
decide	
know	
learn	
move	
	response
solve	
speak	
	training

4 💬 Choose the correct option. Then ask and answer with a partner.
1 What is your greatest **achievement / achieve** in life?
2 What is the best thing about language **learn / learning**?
3 How do you **respond / response** when you find a school subject difficult?
4 What is the best **decision / decide** you have made this year?
5 What **behave / behaviour** do you find really annoying?
6 Who is the cleverest person you **know / knowledge**?

5 🔊 28 Listen to part of the *Your Skilful Brain* podcast and answer the questions.
1 What three rules does Liang Zhao give for keeping teenage brains healthy?
2 What two pieces of advice does Liang give to make learning easier?

82

GRAMMAR

should / shouldn't, must / mustn't

6 🔊 **28** Listen again for examples of *should*, *shouldn't*, *must* and *mustn't*. Then complete the rules.

> 1 We use **should(n't)** / **must(n't)** to give advice.
> 2 We use **should** / **must** to say something is necessary or is a rule.
> 3 We use **shouldn't** / **mustn't** to say something is prohibited or against the rules.

CHECK IT! ➡ **MY GRAMMAR REFERENCE & PRACTICE p118**

7 Complete the advice with *should* or *shouldn't*.
1 You _____ regularly do puzzles. They keep your brain active.
2 You _____ eat lots of junk food. It's not good for your brain.
3 You _____ try to go to bed and wake up at the same time every day.
4 You _____ go somewhere quiet to study, such as a library.
5 You _____ study in front of the TV.
6 You _____ spend too much time alone. Talking and laughing with friends is good for your mental health.

8 Write six rules about the computer room using the information in the sign below. Use *must* and *mustn't*.

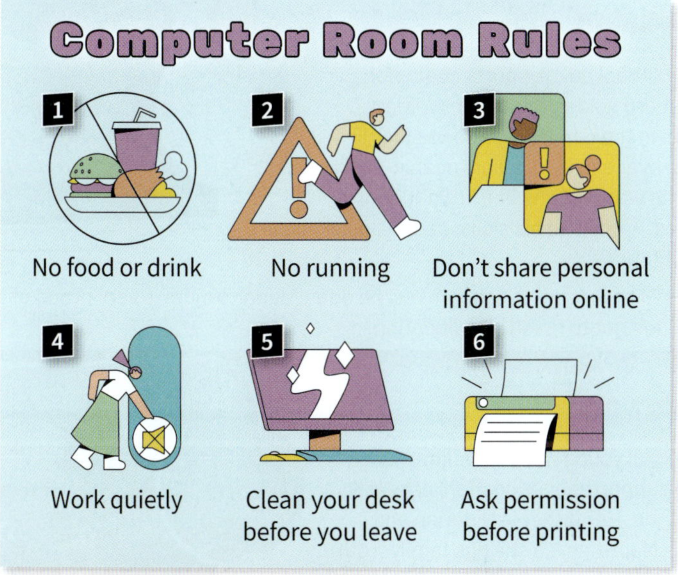

Computer Room Rules

1 No food or drink
2 No running
3 Don't share personal information online
4 Work quietly
5 Clean your desk before you leave
6 Ask permission before printing

9 Complete the rules and advice on learning with *must(n't)* or *should(n't)*. Then match sentences 1–5 to reasons A–E.
1 You _____ cheat in tests.
2 You _____ focus on one thing at a time.
3 You _____ do your homework.
4 You _____ study with other people sometimes.
5 You _____ give up when you fail.

A You learn by repeating things – first at school, then at home.
B Changing from one task to another (and back again) slows you down.
C Failure often comes before success.
D You can discuss things and learn from each other.
E They are an important part of learning.

10 Complete the text with *must(n't)* or *should(n't)* and the verbs in the box.

| copy | do | learn | try | work |

Do you know about Homework Club?

One way for students to study together is Homework Club. There's one at our school on Tuesday and Thursday afternoons – you ¹_____ it sometime.

At Homework Club, there are two rules. Firstly, you ²_____ other people's work. Secondly, you ³_____ together and help each other. You ⁴_____ all your homework at Homework Club though. You ⁵_____ in a variety of ways. Sometimes it's good to study at home on your own.

11 **MEDIATION** Imagine you are introducing an English-speaking exchange student to your school. Write an email to them. Include:
1 two school rules with *must*.
2 two school rules with *mustn't*.
3 two pieces of advice with *should*.
4 two pieces of advice with *shouldn't*.

PROJECT BUILDER 2 Choose your final topic and write some instructions.

➡ **Workbook Project Log p28**

12 👥 Look back at your ideas from Project Builder 1. Choose a final topic and title for your how-to video.

13 👥 Make a list of 5–10 useful words and phrases for your topic.
How to make an English cup of tea: teabag, water, cup, milk, …

14 👥 Write 4–8 instructions with *must(n't)* / *should(n't)* for your video.
First, you must boil the water. Then you should put the teabag in the cup before you add the water.

83

7.3 YOUNG AND SKILFUL

LESSON OBJECTIVES
- Learn about skilful teenagers
- Learn about scanning a text
- Use *have (got) to* to talk about necessity

READING

1 Match pictures A–C in the article with activities 1–3 below.
1. .... e-sports
2. .... film-making
3. .... skateboarding

2 💬 Which of the activities from exercise 1 do you think is the most:
1. interesting? Why?
2. difficult? Why?
3. fun? Why?

3 Read the *Skill UP!* Then read questions 1–5 and decide what kind of information you need to find to answer them.

> **Skill UP!** Scanning is reading quickly to find specific information, e.g. a number, a name, or a place. Work out what kind of information you need to find. Then move your eyes left, right, up and down the text to find it.

What was Zuriel Oduwole's <u>age</u> when she made her first film?

A number.

1. What is Sky Brown's country of birth?
2. What is Jaden Ashman's nationality?
3. What was Sky Brown's age when she had a serious accident?
4. What is Jaden Ashman's gaming name?
5. Where was Zuriel Oduwole born?

4 Scan the article and find the answers to the questions from exercise 3.

What was Zuriel Oduwole's age when she made her first film?

A number: nine.

5 🔊 29 💬 Now read and listen to the article. Then cover it. In pairs, say what you can remember about each teenager.

You don't have to be an adult to be the best!

Check out these super skilful teenagers:

Sky Brown
A

... became the youngest professional skateboarder in the world when she was ten years old. Her mum is Japanese, her dad is British, and Sky was born in Japan. Her Japanese name is Sukai.

Sky is also a talented surfer. She has to get up at 4 a.m. so she can go surfing before school. After school, she practises skateboarding and then surfs again most evenings!

When she was 11, Sky had a serious skateboarding accident and is lucky to be alive. However, she believes you should never give up, and six weeks after the accident Sky was skateboarding again.

Jaden Ashman
B

... is a British school boy, e-sports champion and world-record holder. Jaden, or 'Wolfiez' as he's known in the gaming world, was just 15 when he won over a million dollars at an e-sports event. Now, he plays for one of the world's top gaming teams. Thanks to his skills, Jaden doesn't have to worry about money!

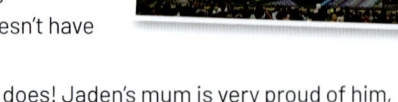

So, does he still have to go to school? Yes, he does! Jaden's mum is very proud of him, but she says he's got to finish his education.

Zuriel Oduwole
C

... is a successful young American film-maker, speaker and supporter of education, especially for girls in Africa. Her father is Nigerian and her mother is Mauritian, so she has family from Africa, but she was born in California. She made her first short documentary film about Africa. It was for a school competition when she was only nine. Since then, she has made several more documentaries. Her films have won awards and appeared in cinemas around the world.

Zuriel has also travelled to many different countries to speak at events about film-making and the power of education, and she has met with over 30 world leaders. Often, she has to work in a world filled with adults. At many of her presentations, she gets the feeling that the people in the audience don't think she's old enough to be presenting. She thinks that might stop when she's in her 20s. But, for now, she enjoys proving to them that young girls like herself can do great things.

6 Answer the questions.
1 Which two sports is Sky Brown very good at?
2 Why does Sky get up so early?
3 How much money did Jaden Ashman win when he was 15?
4 Did Jaden stop going to school after he won?
5 What does Zuriel talk about in her presentations?
6 What feeling does Zuriel often get from her audience during presentations?

7 Find the words in the box in the article. What do they mean in your language?

| proud   successful   talented   top |

GRAMMAR

have (got) to + infinitive without to

8 Complete the table.

Affirmative and negative			
+	I / You / We / They	have to / 've got to	get up at 4 a.m.
-		don't have to / haven't got to	
+	He / She / It	¹ _____ to / got to	
-		² _____ have to / hasn't got to	

Questions		Short answers
Do I	still have to	Yes, I do. / No, I don't.
³ _____ he	⁴ _____ to school?	Yes, he ⁵ _____ . / No, he doesn't.

We use *have (got) to* + infinitive without *to* when we want to say that something is ⁶ **necessary** / **possible**.

We use *don't have to* + infinitive without *to* when we want to say that something is ⁷ **prohibited** / **not necessary**.

Have got to is more ⁸ **informal** / **formal** than *have to*.

CHECK IT! → MY GRAMMAR REFERENCE & PRACTICE p118

9 Complete the sentences with words from the table.
1 Sky Brown _____ to stay fit and healthy.
2 A: _____ Jaden Ashman have to practise video games a lot?
   B: Yes, he _____ .
3 Zuriel Oduwole _____ to be confident to give presentations. Also, she _____ to know a lot about her subject.
4 A: _____ you have to be an adult to be successful?
   B: No, you _____ !
5 An e-sports champion _____ have to go to the gym.

10 Complete the text with the correct forms of *have (got) to* and the verbs in brackets.

Skills4life.edu
#how to do everything!

How to make a successful how-to video

¹ _____ (you / be) a professional to make a successful how-to video? No, you ² _____ (do)! Your video ³ _____ (not win) an Oscar, but there are a few things you ⁴ _____ (get) right. The topic ⁵ _____ (be) interesting and easy to film. The instructions ⁶ _____ (be) simple and clear, and your video ⁷ _____ (be) short. You ⁸ _____ (not write) a script, but you should write some notes. The presenter ⁹ _____ (speak) slowly and with confidence. Don't forget your technical skills! You ¹⁰ _____ (film) your video in a quiet place with lots of light. Make a plan of all the things you ¹¹ _____ (do) before you start and your video will be a success!

11 💬 Talk about things you *have to* and *don't have to* do in these situations.
• you are learning a language
• you are a teacher
• you are rich and famous
• you are a superhero

PROJECT BUILDER 3

Prepare and plan.

→ Workbook **Project Log** p29

12 👥 Read the tasks and discuss what you have to or don't have to do to prepare for your how-to video.
• Find a video camera and other equipment.
• Decide on what pictures or diagrams you want to show.
• Do online research.
• Choose a place to film your video.

13 👥 Do as many of the tasks as you can. Make plans for any tasks that you can't do now and do them later.

> Let's write a list of all the pictures we've got to find.

> OK, then I'll look for them online at home and print copies.

7.4 SHARING SKILLS

LESSON OBJECTIVES
- Learn how young people and their grandparents can benefit from each other
- Focus on using on-screen text in videos
- Learn verbs

LISTENING

1 **Look at photos 1 and 2. What do you think the relationship between the people is? What are they doing?**

2 💬 **Discuss the questions.**
   1 How is spending time together good for grandchildren and grandparents?
   2 What skills and ways of thinking can they learn from each other?

3 ▶Video **Watch the video. Does it mention any of your ideas from exercise 2?**

4 ▶Video **Watch again and choose the correct option.**
   1 According to a study at Oxford, young people who spend time with their grandparents:
      A go to bed earlier.
      B behave better.
      C experience more problems with behaviour.
      D have more emotional problems.
   2 Gemma's grandmother is teaching her how to:
      A bake delicious cakes.
      B use social media.
      C fix her bike.
      D fish.
   3 Research shows that grandparents who support their grandchildren:
      A learn from them.
      B have a better memory.
      C feel happier.
      D live longer.
   4 Jamie says grandparents can teach their grandchildren:
      A about their family history.
      B how to have better memories.
      C about the importance of sharing.
      D how to give good advice.
   5 Which option best describes the main message of the talk?
      A Grandparents are very important to their grandchildren.
      B Grandchildren are very important to their grandparents.
      C Grandparents make good teachers for their grandchildren.
      D Grandparents and grandchildren both benefit from their relationship.

5 ▶Video **Read the Video focus. Then watch again. Which uses of on-screen text 1–6 from the Video focus do you see?**

Video FOCUS — Videos often use on-screen text to:
1 show the video's title.
2 name people, places or things in the video.
3 introduce different sections of the video.
4 give a set of steps or instructions.
5 highlight important words or details in the video.
6 give a summary of the video's main points.
It is not difficult to add on-screen text to a video using video editing software.

Gemma Foster

Jamie Miller

86

VOCABULARY

6 Choose the correct option.
1. Many grandparents find it difficult to **educate** / **communicate** using digital technology, and prefer simple telephone calls.
2. I have **discovered** / **considered** some interesting things about my family by talking to my grandparents.
3. My grandmother is very fit and active – she even **supported** / **offered** to teach me how to ski!
4. My grandfather isn't well and I **expect** / **suggest** he'll come and live with us soon.
5. Grandchildren can **experience** / **provide** fun, love and friendship for their grandparents.

7 Complete the text with the correct forms of the verbs in the box. Which word is not needed? ____

communicate   consider   discover   educate   expect   experience   offer   provide   suggest   support

American grandparents

Research [1] ____ that the average person in the USA can [2] ____ to become a grandparent for the first time at the age of 50. Ninety-six per cent of 65-year-old Americans are grandparents.

According to research, American grandparents feel their most important roles are to [3] ____ their grandchildren about life, and help them [4] ____ their family history. Over a third of grandparents [5] ____ their families by babysitting, and many [6] ____ to help with money when necessary.

Telephone calls are the most common way for grandparents and grandchildren to [7] ____, but almost half of grandparents also use video chat and texting. The most popular thing to do together is to go out and eat.

Nearly all grandparents [8] ____ their relationship with their grandchildren to be good for their health. More than half say they [9] ____ a more active lifestyle and a better social life because of their grandchildren.

8 **MEDIATION** Look online and find three interesting facts about grandparents and grandchildren in your country. Tell the class in English.

9 How many different ways can you think of to complete sentences 1 and 2? Discuss your ideas.
1. The perfect grandparent …
2. The perfect grandchild …

PROJECT BUILDER 4   Share tips and skills with your classmates.

➔ Workbook **Project Log** p29

10 Discuss the questions.
1. Who might be able to provide information to help you with your how-to video, e.g. a grandparent, a teacher, a brother or sister, a friend?
2. Which websites or other sources of information might help you discover more about the topic of your how-to video?

11 Talk to the other students in your class about their how-to videos. Can you offer any tips, suggest any websites or share any skills to help them with their videos? Make a note of any new information.

7.5 GIVING SPOKEN INSTRUCTIONS

LESSON OBJECTIVES • Give spoken instructions • Learn about intonation

SPEAKING

1 ▶ Video Watch the first part of the video. What do Lucy and Marcel show you how to make?

2 ▶ Video Watch again. Number the items of equipment 1–4 in the order Lucy and Marcel use them.
- .... a big plastic bag
- .... ice and salt
- .... warm gloves
- .... a small plastic bag

3 Complete the *Key phrases* with the words in the box.

| before | forget | important | show | sure | thing |

KEY PHRASES

Giving spoken instructions

Starting

I'm / We're going to ¹ .... you how to …
You're going to learn how to …

Talking about equipment / ingredients

² .... you start, …
You will need (to) …
Make ³ .... you (have) …

Making the order of your instructions clear

Step 1 / 2 / 3 is to …
The first / next / final step is to …
The first / next / final ⁴ .... you (have to do) is …
And that's it!

Giving important instructions

It's very ⁵ .... to …   You have to …
Don't ⁶ .... /   You must(n't) …
Remember to … / (Squeeze the bag) like this.

4 🔊 30 Listen to the instructions below. Does the speaker's voice go up or down?
1 Step 1 is to put all the ingredients into one of the small bags.
2 It's very important to close the bags properly.
3 The liquid mustn't come out.

5 Read the *Skill UP!* Then practise saying the instructions in exercise 4 using falling intonation.

> **Skill UP!** We use falling intonation when we want to be very clear about something, e.g. when giving instructions.

6 ▶ Video Look at photos A–C. What mistakes do you think Marcel and Lucy made while making the ice cream? Watch the second part of the video and check.

A

B

C

7 💬 **MEDIATION** Explain how to make one of the dishes below to another pair of students. Use the *Key phrases* and the correct intonation.
- a fruit smoothie
- a healthy salad
- pasta and sauce
- vegetable soup

7.6 CUE CARDS FOR PRESENTING

LESSON OBJECTIVES • Write instructions and cue cards • Learn style tips for writing cue cards

WRITING

1 💬 **Discuss the questions.**
1 How do you feel when you have to speak to a camera or give a presentation?
2 What problems are there if you:
- try to memorize everything?
- read out every word from a script?

2 🔊 **31** Listen to the speaker. Does she mention any of your ideas from exercise 1? Why does she think cue cards are helpful?

3 Look at the cue cards. What is the presentation about? Which example (A or B) is better and why?

A

How to make perfect hot chocolate

Step 1   Ingredients: Before you start you will need milk, sugar, cocoa powder, small pan, cup, spoon.

Step 2   Pour the milk into your cup about three-quarters full. Then pour the milk from the cup into the pan.

B

Perfect Hot Chocolate (1)

STEP 1 – You will need:

Ingredients	Equipment
• milk	• small pan
• sugar	• cup
• cocoa powder	• spoon

(2)

STEP 2 – Pour 3/4 cup of milk into pan:
- Pour milk → into cup
- **3/4 full!**
- Pour milk from cup → into pan

4 Now read the *Skill UP!* and check your ideas from exercise 3.

Skill UP! Writing cue cards
1 Have one main heading, idea or step per card.
2 Write important words only. Don't write full sentences.
3 Write on one side of the card only.
4 Use large, neat writing that is easy to see.
5 Use bullet points, numbers, symbols and colours.
6 Number the cue cards.

5 Read the next part of *How to make perfect hot chocolate*. Write three cue cards based on the text.

STEP 3 is to heat the milk on the stove. When the milk is warm, add the cocoa powder and 1–2 spoons of sugar. The next thing you have to do is to stir the milk slowly and carefully so all the cocoa powder mixes with it. It's very important not to let the milk boil. The final step is to pour the milk back into the cup. Taste it to see if it is sweet enough (add more sugar if not), then enjoy your perfect hot chocolate.

PROJECT BUILDER 5

Write the final instructions and cue cards.

➡ Workbook **Project Log** p30

6 First plan and write the instructions for your how-to video, then write cue cards. Work in groups for Parts A and B only.

A Plan your instructions
- How many steps are in your video? Aim for 3–6.
- What is the main heading for each step?

B Write your instructions
- Write the final instructions for your how-to video.
- Use your work from Project Builders 2 and 4.
- Use the *Key phrases* on page 88 to help you.
- Use *must*, *should* and *have to*.

C Write your cue cards
- Create cue cards to help you when you film your video.
- Follow the advice in the *Skill UP!*

D Read and check
- Check your cue cards are neat and clear.

89

7 PROJECT

Create a how-to video

SHARE AND REVIEW

1. Look back at your Project Builders 1–5 for this unit. Which of the tasks below are new and which are complete?
   - Think of a title for your video.
   - Find the equipment you need.
   - Decide who is doing what.
   - Plan and write the instructions for your how-to video.
   - Write cue cards.
   - Create any pictures or diagrams.
   - Practise.
   - Film.
   - Edit your video and add on-screen text.

Use your Project Log → p28–30

2. Share and review the work from your Project Builders. Is there anything you want to change?

DECIDE

3. Study the diagram below. Complete it with the skills in the box.

   building things   supporting others
   understanding visual information   writing

   Technical skills
   machines, technology, software,
   ....

   Visual skills
   drawing, designing,
   ....

   Word skills
   reading, giving presentations,
   ....

   People skills
   communicating, organizing,
   ....

4. 🔊 32 Listen to Mia, Claire and Ryan talking. Check your answers to exercise 3.

5. What kinds of skills are the different members of your group good at? Use the *Key phrases* to help you.

   KEY PHRASES
   Asking about skills
   - What are you good at?
   - What do you enjoy doing?
   - Who has good (people skills)?
   - You're good with (computers), right?

6. Read the *Project skills*, then decide who will:
   - lead and organize the group.
   - create the pictures and diagrams.
   - present your how-to video.
   - film your how-to video.
   - edit the video and add on-screen text.

   PROJECT SKILLS Teamwork and skills
   Use these tips to help your group work successfully as a team.
   - Find out the skills of each group member.
   - Think about the skills needed for each part of the project.
   - Use this information to decide who does what.
   - Be flexible – project work also offers the chance to develop new skills.

   LIFE SKILLS Thinking about the kinds of skills you are good at will help you make decisions about what to study in the future. What skills do you have? What do you want to study in the future?

CREATE

7 Choose one group member's cue cards from Project Builder 5 and make final copies. Make sure the cards are clear enough for the presenter to read.

8 Practise your how-to video.

9 Read these tips, then film your video:
- Choose high-quality video on your camera / phone.
- Make sure there is enough light on the presenter(s).
- Test the sound and picture quality before you film the whole video.
- If the sound is too quiet, move closer to the presenter(s).
- Move the camera slowly when filming.

10 Edit your video.
- Make sure it is less than five minutes.
- Add some video and audio effects.
- Add some on-screen text.

PROJECT COACH ▶ Video

WATCH AND REACT

11 Watch the other groups' videos. Tick the boxes and add comments to complete it.

	Group 1: ___	Group 2: ___	Group 3: ___
1 The topic was interesting.	☐	☐	☐
2 The instructions were clear.	☐	☐	☐
3 The presenter(s) spoke clearly.	☐	☐	☐
4 The on-screen text was helpful.	☐	☐	☐
5 The visuals, e.g. pictures or diagrams, were useful.	☐	☐	☐
6 The film and sound quality were good.	☐	☐	☐

Comments
7 One thing I really liked about (...)'s video was (...).
8 (...) could improve their video by (...).

REFLECT

12 Think about your project work in this unit. Read the statements and choose your reaction.

COLLABORATION
1 Our group can use our skills to work well as a team.
☹ 😐 🙂 😊 🤩

CREATIVITY
2 Our group can use on-screen text to make videos easy to follow.
☹ 😐 🙂 😊 🤩

COMMUNICATION
3 Our group can present clear instructions to a camera or an audience.
☹ 😐 🙂 😊 🤩

13 Complete these sentences for you.
1 I am pleased with our how-to video because _____
2 I want to improve _____

➔ Workbook **Project Log** p31

8 What a year!

UNIT OBJECTIVES

YOUR PROJECT Create a group yearbook

Project Builders 1–5:
1. Prepare information about memorable events and activities from the school year.
2. Write recommendations for things to do during the school summer holidays.
3. Nominate students for class awards.
4. Prepare information about future jobs.
5. Write a reflective essay about a memorable event.

Read and review each others' yearbooks.

VOCABULARY
- Things to do during the summer holidays
- Jobs

GRAMMAR
- Reflexive and indefinite pronouns
- Question tags

LESSON OBJECTIVES
- Learn vocabulary for talking about school events and activities
- Talk about memorable events and activities from the school year

WARM-UP

1 Look at photos 1–5 from a school yearbook. Match them with five of these school events and activities.
   - .... a guest-speaker talk
   - .... a memorable project (e.g. a science project)
   - .... a school competition (e.g. a spelling competition)
   - .... a school play
   - .... a school trip
   - .... a sports day
   - .... an end-of-year dance
   - .... a school concert

2 Can you add any more school events and activities to the list in exercise 1?

3 **Video** Read about school yearbooks. Then watch Curtis and Amanda's vlog. Which of the underlined features 1–8 in the factfile are in Curtis and Amanda's yearbook?

FACTFILE: School Yearbooks

A school yearbook is a collection of memories, [1] photos, [2] messages and [3] signatures put together by students to help them remember the best parts of the school year and the people they experienced it with.

Yearbooks can be paper or digital. They often contain pages about [4] memorable school events, [5] student awards, and [6] academic achievements. They may also include [7] predictions for students' future jobs and [8] recommendations for things to do in the school holidays.

Curtis and Amanda's VLOG
Looking at our yearbooks

4 **MEDIATION** A friend doesn't speak English. With your partner, explain in your own language what a school yearbook is.

5 **Video** Watch again. Answer the questions.
   1 Where did Curtis's classmates sign their names?
   2 What problem was there at sports day this year?
   3 What does Curtis think of Amanda's performance in the school play?
   4 Where did Curtis and Amanda go for their school trip?
   5 What did the class predict Curtis's future job will be?
   6 What skill does Amanda plan to learn more about during the summer holidays?

PROJECT BUILDER 1
Prepare information for a yearbook section about memorable events and activities from the school year.

→ Workbook **Project Log** p32

6 Choose two or three memorable events or activities from this school year.

7 Complete the table on the right. Answer the questions for each event or activity.

8 At home, look for photos of your memorable events and activities.

	1	2	3
What was the event?	Guest-speaker talk		
When was it?	November		
What happened?	A journalist from a local radio station came to speak to us.		
What do you remember about it?	She was really funny and told us lots of interesting things about working at a radio station.		

8.2 HOLIDAY PLANS

LESSON OBJECTIVES
- Learn vocabulary for talking about things to do during the summer holidays
- Use reflexive pronouns and indefinite pronouns

VOCABULARY

1 💬 Discuss the questions.
1 How do you feel on the last day of the school term?
2 When do your school summer holidays start?
3 How long do they last?

2 💬 Read the web page. Then discuss the questions.
1 Who is the web page for and what is it about?
2 Which is your favourite suggestion on the web page?

3 Make short phrases with the verbs in the box. Use the language from the web page and your own ideas.

arrange	attend	borrow
build	contact	explore
improve	organize	repair
teach		

arrange a day out / a trip / a party
attend a course / a school / a club

4 Using verbs from exercise 3, think of five things that you would like to do during the summer holidays.
arrange a video games competition, borrow some sports equipment …

5 💬 Rank the activities in exercise 4 from most to least interesting. Then compare your answers in pairs.

6 **MEDIATION** Write a text message to an English-speaking friend. Invite them to do the most interesting activity from exercise 5 with you during the holidays. Include at least three pieces of information about your plans, e.g. What? When? Where?

It's nearly the holidays!

We worked hard all year, now it's time to give **ourselves** a break. Here are some fun ways to enjoy the summer holidays.

Be adventurous
Arrange a day out with your family and friends and explore **somewhere** new. Do you own a tent? If not, do you know **anybody** who does? You could borrow it and organize a group camping trip together. Go online and read reviews or contact **someone** you know for advice about the best campsites.

Teach yourself a new skill
Lots of young people use the holidays to teach **themselves something** new! Learn how to rap, dance, fish, act, repair your bike or **anything** else that interests you. Improve your skills by attending an online course, or reading a book.

How do you and your friends keep **yourselves** busy in the holidays?

Comments

Alexandru I got a telescope 🔭 for my birthday so I'm going to teach myself about the stars and planets.

Tanice My sister went to a summer camp last year. She really enjoyed herself.

Yakubu My brother built a BMX ramp all by himself.

Chloe I've got a tent that sets itself up! It makes camping very easy.

GRAMMAR
Reflexive and indefinite pronouns

7 Complete the table. Then find an example of each reflexive pronoun on the web page.

	Subject pronoun	Object pronoun	Reflexive pronoun
Singular	I	me	myself
	you	you	1
	he	him	2
	she	her	3
	it	it	4
Plural	we	us	5
	you	you	6
	they	them	7

8 Choose the correct option to complete the rules.

Reflexive pronouns
- Reflexive pronouns refer back to a person or a thing. We use them when the object is the [1] **same as / different to** the subject of the sentence.
- The phrase (all) [2] **by / on** + reflexive pronoun shows that the subject did something on their own, i.e. without any help.

CHECK IT! ➔ MY GRAMMAR REFERENCE & PRACTICE p120

9 Complete the sentences with the correct reflexive pronouns. Are any of the sentences true for you?
1 I bought a nice present for _____ recently.
2 My friends and I really enjoyed _____ last year in the school summer holidays.
3 My mum and dad decorated our house all by _____ .
4 My pet cleans _____ , so I don't have to do it.
5 My cousin makes some of her clothes _____ .
6 My friend fell off his bike and hurt _____ .

10 💬 Compare your answers to exercise 9 in pairs. Ask and answer follow-up questions.

> 1 is true. I bought a nice present for myself recently.

> Oh really, what?

11 💬 Discuss the questions.
1 How did you keep yourself busy during the last school summer holidays?
2 What new skills would you like to teach yourself during the next school summer holidays?

12 Complete the table with the indefinite pronouns highlighted in the web page.

	Person	Thing	Place
Affirmative	somebody [1]	3	5
Negative / Question	2 anyone	4	anywhere

CHECK IT! ➔ MY GRAMMAR REFERENCE & PRACTICE p120

13 💬 Complete questions 1–3 and instructions 4–6 with the correct indefinite pronouns. Then discuss the questions and follow the instructions in pairs.
1 Did you do _____ interesting during the last school holidays? What?
2 Do you know _____ that doesn't like school holidays?
3 Did you go _____ unusual last summer? Where was it and what did you do there?
4 Tell your partner about _____ you would like to go in the summer holidays.
5 Tell your partner about _____ you would be happy to spend all summer with.
6 Tell your partner about _____ you would like to buy yourself this summer.

PROJECT BUILDER 2

Write recommendations for a yearbook section about things to do during the school summer holidays.

➔ Workbook **Project Log** p32

14 👥 Discuss recommendations for things to do during the school summer holidays. Think of one or two recommendations for each item 1–3.
1 Something for students to learn or teach themselves. What and how?
2 Somewhere for new students to explore. Where and who with?
3 Something students can organize for themselves and their friends or family. What and where?

15 👥 Choose one idea from each item in exercise 14. Then write down your three recommendations.

> If you want to learn something new in the summer holidays, why not teach yourself how to …

8.3 AND THE AWARD GOES TO …

LESSON OBJECTIVES
- Read an online text chat
- Recognize informal style
- Use question tags to ask for agreement or check information

READING

1 Read the headlines below. What do they all have in common?

> **Teens nominate Billie Eilish for a Teen Choice Award**

> Teenage heroes attend BBC Radio 1's Teen Awards ceremony as famous DJs give out awards.

> Greta Thunberg will not accept climate award: *"The climate movement does not need any more awards".*

> **Teenager Lauren Zhang wins Young Musician of the Year award.**

2 What is the difference in meaning between these four phrases?
1 nominate someone for an award
2 win an award
3 give out an award
4 attend an awards ceremony

3 💬 Discuss the questions.
1 Have you or anyone you know ever won an award? What for?
2 Which famous awards ceremonies do you know?

Look UP! Choose a famous awards ceremony and research one of the categories from this year or last year, e.g. The Academy Awards – Best Picture. Find out:
- Which films / people were nominated?
- What / Who won?
- Who gave out the award?

4 🔊 33 Read and listen to the online text chat between Danny, Aymar and Ian. What are they discussing?

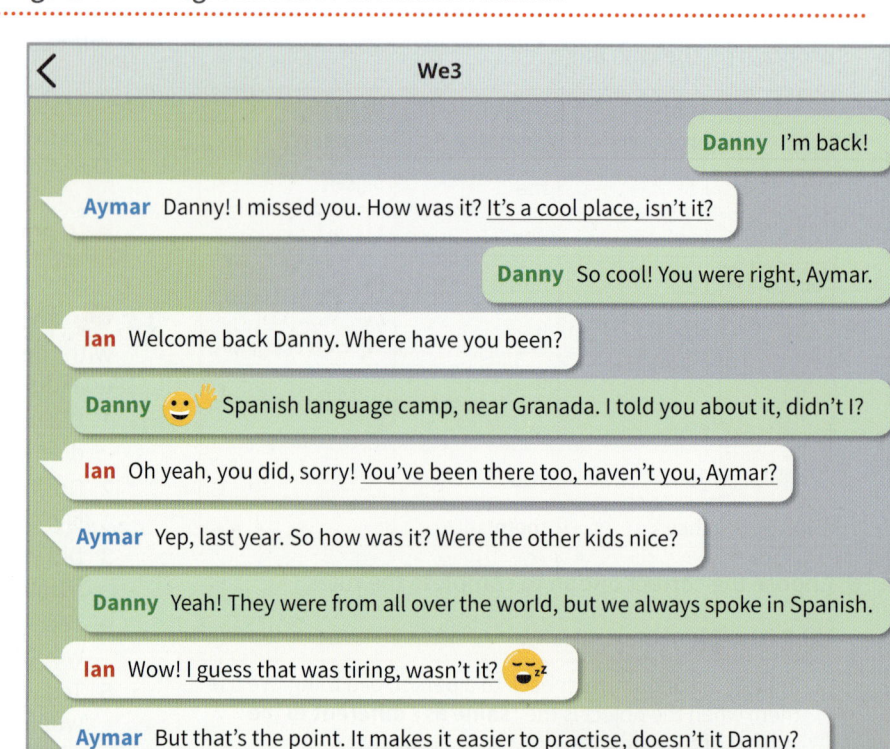

We3

Danny I'm back!

Aymar Danny! I missed you. How was it? It's a cool place, isn't it?

Danny So cool! You were right, Aymar.

Ian Welcome back Danny. Where have you been?

Danny 😄👋 Spanish language camp, near Granada. I told you about it, didn't I?

Ian Oh yeah, you did, sorry! You've been there too, haven't you, Aymar?

Aymar Yep, last year. So how was it? Were the other kids nice?

Danny Yeah! They were from all over the world, but we always spoke in Spanish.

Ian Wow! I guess that was tiring, wasn't it? 😴

Aymar But that's the point. It makes it easier to practise, doesn't it Danny?

Danny It does, but it WAS tiring, Ian. Here's my group. That's Sigrid on the left, and the others. Sigrid was from Norway. She was really cool.

Danny We all nominated people for awards on the last day. I won the 'Human Power Bank' award for the person who's always full of energy!

Human Power Bank
Awarded to
Danny Crowther

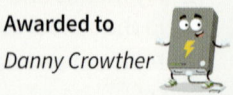

Ian That sounds about right. You don't chill out much, do you Danny? 😂

Danny 💪 Sigrid won the 'Desert Island' award for the person you would most like to be stuck on a desert island with! Everyone liked her. She was so funny.

Aymar So, I guess you won't see Sigrid again, will you?

Danny No, probably not. ☹

Ian You can keep in touch online, can't you?

Danny Well, yes, but …

Aymar Lucky for you Danny, we're funny too, aren't we Ian?

Ian Err … sure! But I'd prefer not to be stuck on an island with either of you, thanks!

5 Read the *Skill UP!* Find examples of features 1–3 in the online text chat on page 96. Then match features 1–3 to their uses A–C.

> **Skill UP!** Understand some of the different features of informal style and why we use them.
> 1 _____ exclamation marks (!), ellipses (…) emojis (☺)
> 2 _____ direct questions, question tags
> 3 _____ exclamations (e.g. *Wow!*), short sentences, phrasal verbs
> A to make writing sound more like speech
> B to express emotions without words
> C to make conversation more personal

6 Are the sentences true (T) or false (F)? Correct the false sentences.
1 Aymar has been to the same language camp as Danny. _____
2 Danny found it tiring to speak Spanish all the time. _____
3 Danny made friends with a Spanish girl called Ingrid. _____
4 Danny won the 'Human Power Bank' award. _____
5 Ian suggests that Danny rarely relaxes. _____
6 Sigrid didn't win an award. _____
7 Danny plans to meet Sigrid again. _____
8 Aymar suggests that Danny is lucky to have funny friends like her and Ian. _____

7 💬 Imagine you are going to an ideal language camp. Describe your plans.

> The language camp is in Italy. I'm going with my best friend for two weeks.

GRAMMAR
Question tags

8 Study the underlined sentences in the online text chat. Then choose the correct options to complete the rules about question tags.

> We use questions tags in speech and ¹ **formal** / **informal** writing to check facts and ask for agreement or confirmation.
> • When the statement is affirmative, use ² **an affirmative** / **a negative** question tag.
> • When the statement is negative, use ³ **an affirmative** / **a negative** question tag.
> • When the statement contains ⁴ **an auxiliary verb** / **a modal verb** (*be*, *have*, *do*) or ⁵ **an auxiliary verb** / **a modal verb** (e.g. *can*, *will*, *should*), repeat it in the question tag.
> • If there isn't an auxiliary verb in the statement, use a form of ⁶ **do** / **be** in the question tag.

CHECK IT! ➡ **MY GRAMMAR REFERENCE & PRACTICE** p120

9 Complete the questions with tags.
1 You've been to a summer camp, _____
2 Danny will miss Sigrid, _____
3 Aymar went to the same camp as Danny, _____
4 You don't know anyone from Norway, _____
5 We should speak English in class, _____
6 Your brother doesn't go to our school, _____
7 We can't meet during the holidays, _____
8 This exercise was easy, _____

10 🔊 **34** Read the *Pronunciation*, then listen and repeat questions 1 and 2 using the correct intonation.

> **PRONUNCIATION** Question tag intonation
> We use falling intonation with a question tag when we expect the speaker to agree with us. We use rising intonation with a question tag when we aren't sure what answer the speaker will give.
> 1 It's a cool place, isn't it? ↘
> 2 You can keep in touch online, can't you? ↗

11 💬 Work with someone you know well. Complete the questions with information about your partner. Then take turns to ask and answer. How many things did you get right?
1 You like _____, don't you?
2 You don't like _____, do you?
3 You will _____, won't you?
4 You won't _____, will you?
5 You can _____, can't you?
6 You have _____, haven't you?
7 You went to _____, didn't you?
8 You think _____, don't you?

PROJECT BUILDER 3

Nominate students for the class awards section of your yearbook.

➡ **Workbook Project Log** p33

12 👥 Nominate classmates for the following awards. Make a note of your choices.
1 **Go-getter:** someone who is always busy
2 **Human Power Bank:** someone with a lot of energy
3 **Human search engine:** someone who knows a lot
4 **Desert Island:** someone people are happy to spend lots of time with
5 **Helpline:** someone who helps other people
6 **Class DJ:** someone who knows a lot about music
7 **Picasso:** someone who is good at drawing
8 **Chill out:** someone who is always calm

> Miguel is always full of energy, isn't he? Let's nominate him for the Human Power Bank award.

97

8.4 DREAM JOBS

LESSON OBJECTIVES
- Focus on questions in videos
- Learn jobs vocabulary
- Learn about matching personal qualities to jobs

LISTENING

1 💬 Discuss the questions.
1 What jobs can you see in photos A–F?
2 How many jobs can you write down in English in one minute?
3 Which jobs on your list would you be good at? Why?
4 What is your dream job? Why?

2 🔊 35 Read the *Video focus*. Then listen to the beginning of an online show. How many questions does the presenter ask the viewers and why?

> **Video FOCUS** Video and television presenters often ask their viewers questions to create interest or drama, or to make a point. The presenters don't usually expect an answer to these kinds of questions.

3 ▶ Video Now watch the video of the complete online show. What is Gemma and Jamie's main point?
A Different jobs are popular in different countries.
B There are different jobs for different people.
C There are lots of unusual jobs in the world.

4 ▶ Video Watch again. Match jobs 1–3 with personalities A–C.
1 ...... panda nanny   A practical people
2 ...... olive oil officer   B caring people
3 ...... water slide tester C people who like making decisions

5 ▶ Video Watch again. Answer the questions.
1 What is Jamie's dream job?
2 Which of the presenters loves animals?
3 Where is the Giant Panda Research Centre?
4 What is Gemma's dream job?
5 What kind of food does Gemma love?
6 Which two jobs does Jamie suggest for musical people?
7 Which three jobs does Gemma suggest for Salima?

6 💬 **MEDIATION** Look online and find out more about the jobs in exercise 4. Which of the jobs would you most like to do and why? Tell a classmate in English.

98

VOCABULARY

7 Match two jobs from the box to each student 1–8. Sometimes more than one answer is possible.

astronaut	baker	builder	cook	dentist	detective	engineer
fashion designer	hairdresser	lawyer	manager	musician	police officer	racing driver
songwriter	video game designer					

1 Devesh Ray — I'm creative and I'd love to work with food.

2 Simon Plummer — I'm musical and I taught myself to play guitar and sing.

3 Camila Garcia — I'm caring and my dream job is something in health or beauty.

4 Tia Wu — I'm active and I'd like to fight crime.

5 Liam Lewis — I'm not musical, but I'd like a creative job.

6 Reva Varma — I'm comfortable taking risks. I'm not scared of anything.

7 Kofi Clark — I like making decisions and telling other people what to do.

8 Annie Richardson — I'm practical and I want a job where I make or build things.

PROJECT BUILDER 4 — Prepare information for a yearbook section about future jobs.

→ **Workbook Project Log** p33

8 What personal qualities do you have? Write down three. Use ideas from exercise 7 or your own.
Creative, practical, …

9 Write three job predictions for yourself based on your personal qualities. Think of:

- a normal job
- an unusual or funny job
- a dream job

10 Read your job predictions to the other members of your group in any order. Can they guess your dream job and give a reason?

> I'd like to be a professional snowboarder, the first astronaut on Mars, or a sports coach. Which one is my dream job?

> I think your dream job is professional snowboarder because I think you're an active person and you're comfortable taking risks.

> Yes! You're right.

8.5 YOU ROCK!

LESSON OBJECTIVES • Express and respond to thanks • Respond to thanks with *Thank YOU*

SPEAKING

1 💬 Discuss the questions.
1 Can you explain what 'thank you' means, using English?
2 When do we thank people formally and when informally? Give an example of each.
3 Why is it important to thank people?

2 ▶Video Watch the first part of the video. What school event are Amy, Marcel and Lucy preparing for, and how?

3 ▶Video Complete the table with the words in the box. Then watch again and check.

| appreciate | best | grateful | million |
| pleasure | problem | rock | thank |

KEY PHRASES
Expressing and responding to thanks

Expressing thanks

That's (nice / kind) of you.
I'd like to ¹_____ you for …
I'm very ²_____ for …
Thanks (so much) for everything.
I really ³_____ (it).

Fun informal ways to say thank you

You're the ⁴_____!
You ⁵_____!
Thanks a lot / a ⁶_____!
I owe you one!

Responding to thanks

No ⁷_____.
My ⁸_____.
You're (very) welcome.
Don't mention it.

LIFE SKILLS Remember the power of saying *thank you*. People respond positively, even when you thank them for small things. Saying thank you is a great way to build new relationships and look after old ones. Think of examples of small things you can thank people for.

4 ▶Video Look at the photo. What award do you think Amy won? Watch the second part of the video and check.

5 Complete the two conversations. Use words from the *Key phrases*.

• **Mario** It was a great party, Abi. You ¹_____!
  Abi My ²_____, Mario. And thanks a ³_____ for my cool present. That was very ⁴_____ of you.
  Mario You're very ⁵_____. Happy birthday one more time!

• **Paco** I really ⁶_____ your help, Julia, and I'm very ⁷_____ for your advice.
  Julia Don't ⁸_____ it, Paco. That's what friends are for!

6 🔊 36 Read the *Skill UP!* Then listen to a conversation. What is Antonia thanking Emilio for?

Skill UP Sometimes people thank us, but we feel we should be saying thank you to THEM. In these situations, you can say *No, thank YOU*, with stress on the word 'you'.

7 💬 Read the three situations. Then take turns expressing thanks and responding to it. Use appropriate (formal or informal) *Key phrases*.

Student A
• Student B is awarding you first prize (€1,000) for winning a competition. A large audience is watching.
• Student B is an older adult and your neighbour. They looked after your cat when you were on holiday.
• Student B is your best friend. They baked you a birthday cake.

Student B
• Student A is awarding you a prize for raising money for charity. You are on television.
• Student A is your friend's mother or father. You went on holiday with their family this year.
• Student A is your best friend. They bought you a great present for your birthday.

100

8.6 AN EVENT TO REMEMBER

LESSON OBJECTIVES • Write a reflective essay • Learn how to organize information in a reflective essay

WRITING

1 Which three places would you like to visit for a school trip? Why?
- a fire station
- a historical building
- a science museum
- a sports stadium
- a television studio
- an airport
- an art gallery
- an outdoor activity centre
- a theatre
- a farm

2 Read Lotte's reflective essay and answer the questions.
1 What type of place did Lotte and her class visit on their school trip?
2 What did Lotte learn on the school trip?
3 What decision did Lotte make as a result of the trip?

3 Read the essay again. Which paragraph:
A ...... describes the memorable event?
B ...... tells you what the essay will be about?
C ...... describes what Lotte enjoyed most about the event.
D ...... gives a summary of the essay?
E ...... describes what Lotte learned from the event?

4 Read the *Skill UP!* Check your answers to exercise 3.

> **Skill UP!**
> **Writing a reflective essay**
> Organize your essay into five paragraphs:
> 1 Introduction: Explain what your essay is about.
> 2 Paragraph 2: Describe the memorable event.
> 3 Paragraph 3: Say what you enjoyed about the event.
> 4 Paragraph 4: Say what you learned from the memorable event.
> 5 Conclusion: Summarize your main points.

5 Study the underlined language in the essay. Find:
1 a phrase to help you describe the best part of the event.
2 four phrases to help you describe what you learned from the event.
3 a phrase to help you summarize your essay.
4 a phrase to help you explain what your essay is about.

---

1 <u>In this essay, I will</u> describe a memorable event from this school year and explain what it taught me.

2 In October, my class went on a school trip to the NEMO science museum, in Amsterdam. We spent a very memorable day there visiting all the different exhibitions and learning about science.

3 <u>My favourite part</u> of the science museum was the laboratory. We dressed like scientists and did our own chemistry experiments.

4 The visit was really fun and <u>taught me</u> some important things about science. <u>I learned</u> that chemistry is very important for understanding what everything in the world is made of. I decided that I would like to study and work in science in the future.

5 <u>In conclusion</u>, our school trip to NEMO was memorable, and also very valuable for me. It <u>showed me</u> how important science is and <u>helped me</u> think about my future career.

PROJECT BUILDER 5

Write a reflective essay about a memorable event and what you learned from it.

→ Workbook **Project Log** p34

6 Write a reflective essay for your yearbook.

A Plan
- What memorable event do you want to write about? You could look back at Project Builder 1 for ideas.
- What did you enjoy about the event?
- What did you learn from the event?

B Write
- Follow the tips in the *Skill UP!* and write your essay.

C Read and check
- Check that your essay is organized into five paragraphs.
- Check your spelling and grammar.

8 PROJECT

Create a group yearbook

SHARE AND REVIEW

1 Look back at your Project Builders 1–5 for this unit. In which Project Builder did you:
   - A write about memorable events and activities from the school year? 1
   - B nominate students for class awards? ......
   - C write recommendations for things to do during the school summer holidays? ......
   - D write a reflective essay about a memorable event? ......
   - E write job predictions for yourself? ......

2 Share and review the work from your Project Builders. Is there anything you want to change?

Use your Project Log → p32–34

DECIDE

3 Match features 1–7 to pictures A–G. In which sections of your yearbook could you use these features and how?
   1 ...... a calendar / year plan
   2 ...... a group photo
   3 ...... icons
   4 ...... photos or graphics found online
   5 ...... a quotation or message for your class
   6 ...... signatures
   7 ...... bullet points

B *Don't be sad because it's over; smile because it happened.*

4 Now read these tips for creating your yearbook. Do they mention any of your ideas from exercise 3?

MEMORABLE EVENTS AND ACTIVITIES SECTION
- Create this using the information in your tables from Project Builder 1, plus any photos you found. You can also add your group's essays from Project Builder 5 here.
- **TIP** Organize this section around a calendar or year plan of important dates.

SCHOOL SUMMER HOLIDAYS SECTION
- Include your recommendations for things to do during the school summer holidays from Project Builder 2.
- **TIP** Find some pictures and graphics online to illustrate this section. Use bullet points for the text.

CLASS AWARDS SECTION
- Include your nominations for awards from Project Builder 3.
- **TIP** Use icons to represent the awards and to make this section look attractive.

FUTURE JOBS SECTION
- Include your group's personal qualities and all the predictions for your future jobs from Project Builder 4.
- **TIP** Take a group photo, then write everyone's names and job predictions around it.

EXTRA! You might want to leave a page at the end of your yearbook for your classmates to sign their names and write some messages.

5 Decide who will prepare each section of your group yearbook.

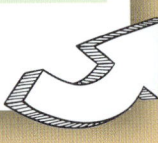

102

CREATE

6 Read the *Project skills*. Make decisions as a group about the design of your yearbook.

PROJECT SKILLS Thinking about design
- Choose one or two fonts and use them on all pages.
- Use **bold**, *italics* and **different sizes** for emphasis.
- Choose three or four colours and use them on all pages.
- Use a similar design and layout for each page of your project.

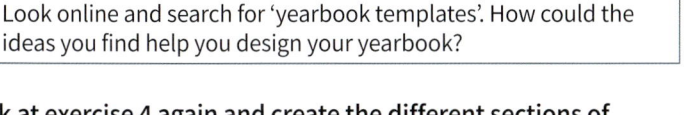

PROJECT COACH ▶ Video

Look UP! Look online and search for 'yearbook templates'. How could the ideas you find help you design your yearbook?

7 Look at exercise 4 again and create the different sections of your yearbook. Then put everyone's work together into one book.

READ AND REACT

8 Leave your yearbook on a classroom table and walk around in your group, looking at the other groups' yearbooks. Think about the questions below.
1. Did any of the groups write about the same memorable event(s) as you?
2. Which summer holiday recommendations sound interesting? Why?
3. How are the other groups' award nominations similar or different to your group's?
4. What jobs did other groups predict for themselves? Would you like to do any of these jobs?
5. Write a message and sign your name in the other groups' yearbooks.

REFLECT

9 Think about your project work in this unit. Read the statements and choose your reaction.

COLLABORATION
1. Our group can share tasks and work together to make a yearbook.

CREATIVITY
2. Our group can design an attractive yearbook.

COMMUNICATION
3. I can communicate about past events in speech and in writing.

10 Complete these sentences for you.
1. I am pleased with our yearbook because
2. I want to improve

➔ Workbook **Project Log** p35

103

0 MY GRAMMAR REFERENCE AND PRACTICE

Question words

- We use different question words to ask for different types of information.

Question word	Use
What	To ask about things and actions
Where	To ask about places
When	To ask about times
Which	To ask about things and people
Who	To ask about people
Why	To ask about reasons
How	To ask about the way to do something; to ask about amounts

- We can form questions in the present simple with *be*.
What colour is the jacket?

- We also form questions in the present simple with:
Question word + *do* / *does* + subject + verb + ?
How do I get to the museum?

Question word	*do* / *does* + subject	Verb	
What	do I	want	for dinner?
Where	do you	live?	
When	do we	get	home?
Which	do they	prefer?	
Who	does he	live	with?
Why	does she	like	shopping?
How	does it	work?	

1 Complete each question with one question word.
1 'Why is your hair wet?' 'It's raining.'
2 '............ does he get home every day?' 'By train.'
3 '............ is her birthday?' 'It's on 13th June.'
4 '............ do you need?' 'A pencil and some paper.'
5 '............ is the cinema?' 'It's on Plum Street.'
6 '............ does she sit next to in class?' 'Her friend Mila.'
7 '............ is your food?' 'It's very nice, thank you.'
8 '............ ice cream do you prefer? Strawberry or chocolate?'

like + -ing / noun

- We use *like* + *-ing* to give opinions about activities:
My sister (doesn't) like playing video games.

- We can use *like* + noun to give opinions about things, people or places:
I (don't) like burgers / my teacher / New York.

- For questions and answers:

like + *-ing*	Answers
Do you like playing tennis?	Yes, I do. I love it.
Does he like playing piano?	No, he doesn't. He hates it.
like + noun	Answers
Do they like pizza?	Yes, they do. They're crazy about it.
Does she like dogs?	No, she doesn't. She can't stand them.

- We use these verbs and phrases in the same way as *like*:

+	love, be crazy about
+ / -	don't mind
-	hate, can't stand

My brother's crazy about football.

2 Write present simple sentences with *-ing* / noun.
1 Grace / love / travel to different countries
   Grace loves travelling to different countries.
2 I / can't stand / spiders
3 we / not mind / study for exams
4 Connor / hate get up / early
5 Holly / like / pasta with cheese

Quantifiers

	With countable nouns	With uncountable nouns
Affirmative	There are **some** / **a lot of** cars.	There is **some** / **a lot of** water.
Negative	There aren't **any** / **many** / **a lot of** / **enough** chairs.	There isn't **any** / **much** / **a lot of** / **enough** time.
Questions	How **many** books have you got?	How **much** money do we need?
	Do you have **any** / **a lot of** / **enough** books?	Do you have **any** / **a lot of** / **enough** time?

3 Choose the correct option.
1 Be careful. There's **any** / **some** ice on the road.
2 How **many** / **much** carrots do you want?
3 Do you have **any** / **many** sugar?
4 I haven't got **some** / **any** money in my pocket.
5 There aren't **enough** / **a lot of** eggs for an omelette. I've only got one.
6 There's not **many** / **much** food in the fridge.

Present simple

- We use the present simple to talk about routines and habits.
  I study every day.
- We also use the present simple to talk about facts, feelings and opinions.
  He doesn't speak French.
- With negative forms, we don't add -s or -es to the verb with *he / she / it*.
  She doesn't eat meat. (NOT: ~~She doesn't eats meat.~~)

Affirmative		
I / You / We / They	like	milk.
He / She / It	likes	
Negative		
I / You / We / They	don't like	chips.
He / She / It	doesn't like	
Questions	**Short answers**	
Do you like ice cream?	Yes, I do. / No, I don't.	
Does he like tomatoes?	Yes, he does. / No, he doesn't.	

4 Choose the correct option.
1. My parents **live** / **lives** in New Zealand.
2. Elsa **work** / **works** in a library.
3. Greg and Selma **study** / **studies** Chinese at school.
4. Does Sophie **go** / **goes** horse riding at the weekend?
5. My best friend **play** / **plays** the guitar and the piano.

Present continuous

- We use the present continuous to talk about actions happening now (or not) or around the time of speaking. We form the present continuous with *am / are + -ing*.
- We form *yes/no* questions in the present continuous with:
  Am / Are / Is + subject + *-ing* form

Affirmative		Negative
I	am / 'm	speaking English.
He / She / It	is / 's	
You / We / They	are / 're	
Negative		
I	am / 'm not	listening to music.
He / She / It	is not / isn't	
You / We / They	are not / aren't	
Questions		
Am I		wearing a hat?
Is he / she / it		
Are you / we / they		

- In affirmative short answers, we don't use short forms.
  'Are you reading?' 'Yes, I am.' / 'No, I'm not.' (NOT: ~~Yes, I'm.~~)

5 Complete the sentences. Use the present continuous form of the verbs in brackets.
1. You <u>aren't listening</u> (not / listen) to me.
2. _____ they _____ (watch) the news?
3. I _____ (not / enjoy) the film.
4. She _____ (study) English at college.
5. Why _____ they _____ (smile)?

Present continuous: future arrangements

- An arrangement is a plan with a fixed time and/or place. It often includes other people. We can use the present continuous to talk about arrangements.
  We're meeting at the cinema on Saturday.
  Are you getting the seven o'clock flight?

6 Write questions with the present continuous. Then match them to answers A–E.
1. where / you go / this evening?
   Where are you going this evening? C
2. what time / Leah leave?
3. you / run / on Sunday morning?
4. how long / they / stay / at Grandma's / in July?
5. when / Mike and Jane / get married?

A Yes, I am. Do you want to join me?
B In August.
C I'm going to the cinema with Suzi.
D They're staying for two weeks.
E She's leaving at 4 p.m.

Possessive pronouns

Subject pronoun	I	you	he	she	it	we	they
Possessive adjective	my	your	his	her	its	our	their
Possessive pronoun	mine	yours	his	hers	–	ours	theirs

7 Complete the sentences with a possessive pronoun from the table.
1. 'This isn't my book. Is it <u>yours</u>?' 'Yes, it is. Thanks.'
2. Brad doesn't like milk, so I'm sure this drink isn't _____.
3. The blue suitcase is _____. We lost it last week.
4. It's not Katy's phone. _____ is black.
5. 'Is that your parents' car?' 'The red one? Yes, that's _____.'

REMEMBER! Never use an apostrophe with a possessive pronoun: *'My bag is next to your's.'* ✗
'My bag is next to yours.' ✓

105

1 MY GRAMMAR REFERENCE AND PRACTICE

Past simple: regular and irregular verbs

- We use the past simple to talk about states or completed actions in the past.
  Ella was relaxed before the game.
  Euro Disney opened in 1992.

- We use it for repeated actions and things that happened one after another.
  She checked her phone about ten times during the meal!
  He got into the car, shut the door, and started the engine.

- We add *-ed* to form the past simple of most regular verbs.

Past simple: regular verbs		
Most verbs	add *-ed*	play → played
Ends in *-e*	add *-d*	live → lived
Ends in a consonant + *-y*	change *-y* to *-ied*	study → studied
Most verbs ending in one vowel + one consonant (except *w* and *y*)	double the consonant and add *-ed*	stop → stopped

- The past simple verb form is the same for every subject (*I, you, he, she*, etc.) except for the verb *be*:
  She wore sunglasses. (NOT: ~~She wores sunglasses.~~)

Was and *were* are the past simple forms of the verb *be*.

Past simple: *be*		
	Affirmative	Negative
I / He / She / It	was	wasn't
You / We / They	were	weren't

- With irregular verbs, we do not add *-ed* for the past simple form. They all have different forms.

  buy → bought leave → left see → saw
  eat → ate make → made swim → swam
  give → gave put → put write → wrote

  → Irregular verb list p127–128

- We form negatives and questions in the same way for regular and irregular verbs, except for the verb *be* and modal verbs (*can, must*, etc.).

Negatives			
Subject	*didn't* (*did not*)	Infinitive without *to*	
I / He / She / It / You / We / They	didn't	come	to the party.

Questions				
Question word	*did*	Subject	Infinitive without *to*	
When	did	you	get	home?
	did	she	write	to you?

- The main verb in negatives and questions is the infinitive without *to* (*play*), not the past simple form (*played*).
  I didn't finish my work. (NOT: ~~I didn't finished my work.~~)
  Did you fly to Tokyo? (NOT: ~~Did you flew to Tokyo?~~)

- In short answers, we use *did* or *didn't*.
  'Did you meet her parents?' 'Yes, I did.' / 'No, I didn't.'

  These forms are the same for both regular and irregular verbs, except for the verb *be*.

- We can also answer a *yes/no* question with just *yes* or *no*.
  'Did you see the castle?' 'Yes.' / 'No.'

- We pronounce the *-ed* endings of regular verbs in the past simple in different ways.

Pronunciation: regular verbs ending in *-ed*		
Verbs that end in a voiced sound, except /d/	pronounce *-ed* as /d/	play**ed** (/pleɪd/) liv**ed** (/lɪvd/)
Verbs that end in an unvoiced sound*, except /t/	pronounce *-ed* as /t/	work**ed** (/wɜːkt/) stopp**ed** (/stɒpt/)
Verbs that end in the sound /d/ or /t/	pronounce *-ed* as /ɪd/	end**ed** (/endɪd/) start**ed** (/stɑːtɪd/)

*Sounds that don't require our voices (only air) are called 'unvoiced': /p/, /t/, /tʃ/, /k/, /f/, /θ/, /s/, /ʃ/, /h/

Past simple: (*there*) *was* / *were*

- We use *there was* / *were* to talk about things in the past.
  There was a record shop on the high street.
  There were lots of people at the concert.

Past time phrases

- We often use past time phrases with the past simple to say exactly when things happened, e.g. *an hour ago, at lunchtime, yesterday, last week, in 2017, ten years ago*.
  I saw Bella an hour ago.
  They didn't go to the lake yesterday.
  Was it hot last week?

REMEMBER! With past simple negatives, we usually use the short form *didn't*, but we sometimes use the full form *did not* in formal writing.

1 Complete the sentences. Use the correct past simple form of the verbs in brackets.
1 Richard <u>left</u> (leave) school in 2006.
2 My parents _____ (have) a house by the sea.
3 We _____ (not / see) our cousins last week.
4 _____ (they / go) to Spain in June?
5 When _____ you _____ (arrive)?
6 I _____ (stop) working at 9 p.m.
7 They _____ (organize) a surprise party for us.
8 When _____ the film _____ (finish)?

2 Correct the sentences.
1 What time you woke up?
   What time did you wake up?
2 My grandfather didn't had green eyes.
3 I tidied the house. After then, I made lunch.
4 We played tennis from 9.30 and 12.30.
5 I didn't kept the letter.
6 When you did meet Sophie?
7 Lily lived here during six years.
8 Harry arrived lunchtime.

3 Complete the dialogue.
A Hi Johan, did you go out last night?
B Yes, I ¹<u>did</u>. I went to the cinema.
A What did you ² _____ ?
B *Tenet*.
A I don't know that film. ³ _____ you like it?
B No, I ⁴ _____ . It was very long. How about you? ⁵ _____ did you do last night?
A I listened to some old vinyl.
B Really?! Where ⁶ _____ you buy that?
A I ⁷ _____ it at the old record shop on the high street.
B ⁸ _____ did it open?
A It opened a year ⁹ _____ !

4 Complete the text with the correct form of the words in the box.

| enjoy | not last | not look | perform | play | show |
| think | travel | wear | | | |

When my dad was at school, he ¹<u>played</u> the guitar in a band. The band usually ² _____ at the school disco and they sometimes ³ _____ to other schools, too. They ⁴ _____ jeans with holes in them and baggy T-shirts and they ⁵ _____ they looked cool. Dad ⁶ _____ me a photo – they ⁷ _____ very fashionable (in my opinion!). The band ⁸ _____ very long, but Dad really ⁹ _____ it.

5 Complete the sentences. Use the correct form of *there was/wasn't* or *there were/weren't*.
1 <u>Was there</u> a message from Alice on the phone?
2 _____ a gym in the town in those days.
3 _____ any people swimming in the sea yesterday.
4 'Was there an airport on the island?' 'No, _____ .'
5 _____ many people at the party.
6 _____ any good DVDs at the second-hand shop?
7 In the room _____ one big desk and two chairs.
8 The test was great! _____ some really easy questions.

6 Match sentence halves 1–8 to A–H.
1 He posted the letter on <u>C</u>
2 We bought a new car last _____
3 I first met Sandra three years _____
4 The journey only took _____
5 Barack Obama was president of the USA from _____
6 The accident happened at _____
7 Did you see Layla _____
8 My parents listened to vinyl in the _____

A 20 minutes.   E ago.
B 2009 to 2017.   F 1990s.
C Monday.   G about ten o'clock.
D yesterday?   H month.

7 Complete the text with the correct form of the words in the box.

| <s>be</s> | buy | get | know | sell | spend | there are |
| there is | | | | | | |

When I ¹<u>was</u> a teenager, ² _____ a music shop in the town centre. It sold vinyl, cassettes and CDs. It didn't only ³ _____ music from the top 40 of the time, but music from the 60s and 70s, too. On Saturdays, I ⁴ _____ the bus into town and ⁵ _____ hours looking for singles (one song on one record) and listening to music. ⁶ _____ shop assistants to help you and they ⁷ _____ everything about all types of music. Now things are very different – I don't have to get the bus into town to choose a single – I download it. Last week, I ⁸ _____ three new albums without leaving the house – this is great news at my age!

107

2 MY GRAMMAR REFERENCE AND PRACTICE

Past continuous

- We use the past continuous to talk about actions in progress at a time in the past.
  I was watching TV at ten o'clock last night.

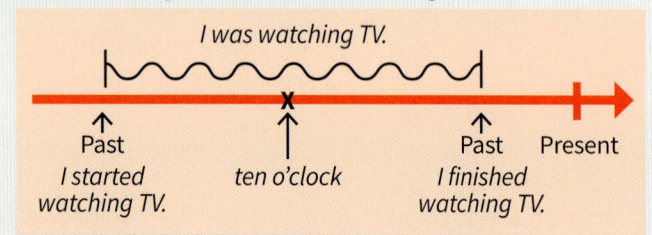

- We often use the past continuous to describe a scene, especially at the start of a story.
  The sun was shining and the birds were singing.

- We also use the past continuous for an action that continues for a whole period of time, e.g. a day or week.
  I was working on my project all week.

- We form the past continuous with:
  Subject + *was* / *were* + *-ing* form of the verb

Affirmative and negative			
Subject	was / were	-ing form	
+	I / He / She / It	was	running	in the park.
	You / We / They	were	eating	in a restaurant.
−	I / He / She / It	wasn't	moving	very fast.
	You / We / They	weren't	playing	video games.

- To form questions, we change the order of *was* / *were* and the subject:
  Was / *Were* + subject + *-ing* form
  Question word + *was* / *were* + subject + *-ing* form

Questions				
Question word	was / were	Subject	-ing form	
	Was	I / he / she / it	running	in the park?
	Were	you / we / they	eating	in a restaurant?
Why	was	the bus	going	the wrong way?
What	were	the children	doing?	

- We can answer *yes*/*no* questions with short answers.
  'Was he running in the park?' 'Yes, he was.' / 'No, he wasn't.'

- We don't usually use the past continuous with state verbs such as *believe*, *need* and *understand*, but we often use it with verbs which show that the action or event lasted a long time, such as *wait*, *live*, *work* and *rain*.
  They were living in Paris last year.

Past continuous and past simple

- We use the past continuous when an action in the past is interrupted or unfinished. We use the past simple for finished actions in the past. Compare these two sentences:
  I was reading my book on the train. (= I didn't finish it.)
  I read the magazine on the train. (= I read the whole magazine.)

- We can use the past simple and the past continuous together for actions that happened at the same time. We use the past continuous for the longer action and the past simple for the shorter action.
  I was sitting on the train when I phoned my mum.

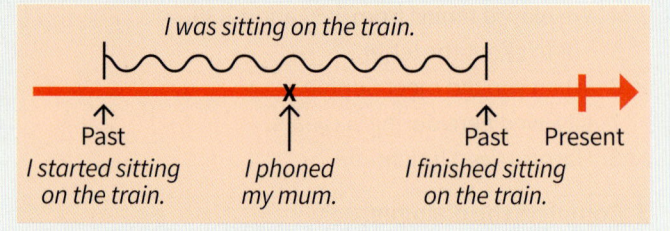

- We can put the past continuous before the past simple in a sentence or we can put the past simple first.

Past continuous	Past simple
I was sitting on the train	when I phoned my mum.
Past simple	**Past continuous**
I phoned my mum	while I was sitting on the train.

- We usually use the past simple to describe past states.
  I hated carrots when I was a child. (NOT: *I was hating carrots when I was a child.*)

Connecting past actions with *as*

- We can also use the past continuous with two actions in the same sentence. It expresses the idea that both actions were happening at the same time. We often use *as* to show this.
  As we were eating dinner, Ali was doing her homework.

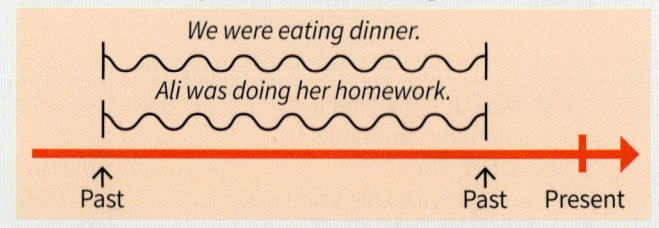

> **REMEMBER!** We often use *when* before the past simple and *while* before the past continuous.

1 **Complete the sentences. Use the past continuous form of the verbs in brackets.**
   1 At seven o'clock yesterday evening, I was watching (watch) a musician at the town hall.
   2 Why _____ (you / take) photos of that building?
   3 You _____ (not listen) to me while I _____ (speak) to you!
   4 Verity _____ (walk) along the street, _____ (eat) an ice cream.
   5 Ben _____ (watch) TV and Toby _____ (paint) a picture.
   6 At eleven o'clock, Elijah _____ (play) video games.

2 **Complete the text with the past continuous form of the verbs in the box.**

   | eat | finish | get | ~~look~~ | talk | watch |

   It was a busy morning. Mum ¹was looking for her bag and Dad ² _____ his breakfast and ³ _____ the news on TV. I ⁴ _____ my homework and my brother ⁵ _____ to his friend on the phone. We ⁶ _____ ready for the day.

3 **What were you doing at these times yesterday? Write true sentences for you.**
   I was sleeping at 6 a.m.
   1 6 a.m.   3 12.30 p.m.   5 9 p.m.
   2 11 a.m. 4 7 p.m.   6 10.30 p.m.

4 **Choose the correct option.**
   1 A **Did it snow** / **Was it snowing** when you woke up this morning?
     B Yes, everything was white when I **opened** / **was opening** the curtains.
   2 A What time **did you get** / **were you getting** home yesterday?
     B Eight o'clock. John's dad **drove** / **was driving** me home.
   3 A I **saw** / **was seeing** you this morning.
     B Really? Where was I? What **did I do** / **was I doing**?
   4 A **Did you enjoy** / **Were you enjoying** your trip? What was London like?
     B Very crowded and busy! Everyone **rushed** / **was rushing** around!
   5 A What **did you do** / **were you doing** after school yesterday?
     B I **met** / **was meeting** my friends and we **went** / **were going** to the park.
   6 A I **phoned** / **was phoning** you at five o'clock, but you didn't answer.
     B Sorry, I **talked** / **was talking** to my friend Harry.
   7 A When **did you move** / **were you moving** to this town?
     B We **came** / **were coming** here about five years ago.

5 **Complete the text with the correct form of the words in the box.**

   | enjoy | have | knit | paint | see | ~~not understand~~ |
   | walk | want | | | | |

   1 I tried to answer the question, but I didn't understand it.
   2 While we were living there, Josie _____ a serious accident and hurt her back.
   3 A Carla called while you were out.
     B Oh, do you know what she _____?
   4 I saw an amazing street artist in town. He _____ on a wall.
   5 My son spent six months in Spain and he really _____ it.
   6 My grandma _____ when I arrived for tea.
   7 _____ you _____ in the mountains when you took that photo?
   8 We were walking home when we _____ a sculpture in the park.

6 **Write sentences with the past continuous and as.**
   1 I was taking a photo and the celebrity came out of the restaurant.
   As I was taking a photo, the celebrity came out of the restaurant.
   2 I was dancing and Livvy sang.
   3 I drove. It was snowing.
   4 I wrote my essay. My sister painted a picture.
   5 She was having breakfast. Her brother got dressed.

7 **Complete the text with the past simple or past continuous form of the verbs in brackets.**

   Yesterday afternoon, I ¹was walking (walk) home from school through the town centre when I ² _____ (see) a lot of people. So I ³ _____ (stop) to see what ⁴ _____ (happen). A group of street dancers ⁵ _____ (perform) and people ⁶ _____ (clap). They were amazing. While I ⁷ _____ (watch) them, people ⁸ _____ (film) it. When I got home, I ⁹ _____ (tell) my brother about it and he said they were his friends!

109

3 MY GRAMMAR REFERENCE AND PRACTICE

will / won't for predictions

- We use *will* and *won't* to make predictions about the future.
  I'm sure she'll win the match tomorrow.
  We won't see them again this year.
- The form of *will* or *won't* is the same for every subject (*I, you, it, they*, etc.).
- We use the infinitive without *to* in both affirmative and negative forms.
  Pete won't be early. (NOT: *Pete won't to be late.*)

Affirmative and negative			
	Subject	will / won't	Infinitive without *to*	
+	I / He / She / It / You / We / They	will / 'll	make	lots of money in the future.
			be	happy.
−	I / He / She / It / You / We / They	will not / won't	stay	here for long.
			go	on holiday next year.

- To form *yes/no* questions, we change the order of the subject and *will*.

Will	Subject	Infinitive without *to*	
Will	I / he / she / it / you / we / they	make	lots of money in the future?
Short answers			
Yes, I will. / No, I won't.			

- To form *Wh-* questions, the question word goes at the beginning of the question, before *will*.
  How will people travel in the year 3000? (NOT: *People will how travel in the year 3000?*)

Question word	will	Subject	Infinitive without *to*	
When	will	you	make	lots of money?
How			do	it?

- In spoken English, we usually use the short form of *will* with personal pronouns (e.g. *I'll, you'll, he'll, she'll*). In the negative, we usually use the short form *won't*. We use *won't* in negative short answers, too (e.g. *No, I won't.*).

> **REMEMBER!** We don't use the short form in affirmative short answers:
> *'Will Sunita be there?'*
> *'Yes, she'll.'* ✗ *'Yes, she will.'* ✓

First conditional

- We use the first conditional to talk about a possible action or situation in the future, and the result or effect that follows.
  If I have time this afternoon, I'll plant some flowers.
  If clause = *If I have time this afternoon,*
  Result clause = *I'll plant some flowers.*
- We form the first conditional with the *if* clause + result clause (or result clause + *if* clause).
- We form the *if* clause with *If* + subject + present simple. We form the result clause with subject + *will*('ll) / *will not* (*won't*) + infinitive without *to*.

Affirmative, negative and *yes/no* questions					
	If	Subject	Present simple	Subject + will / won't	Infinitive without *to*	
+	If	Luke	visits us,	we'll	take	him to London.
−	If	you	don't study harder,	you won't	pass	that exam.
?	If	I	leave before dinner,	will	they	mind?

- We can also ask first conditional questions using question words.
  How will you get to the beach if we go?
  What will they do if the park closes?
- We can put the *if* clause before or after the result clause. We use a comma after the *if* clause when it comes before the result clause.

if clause / action	Result
If I see Cathy,	I'll invite her for dinner.
If I see Cathy,	I'll give her the message.

Result	*if* clause / action
I'll invite Cathy for dinner	if I see her.
I'll give Cathy the message	if I see her.

1 **Complete the sentences with** *'ll, will* **or** *won't* **and the verbs in the box.**

| be   not be   ~~not go~~   not have   live   see   start |
| tell |

1 Children **won't go** to school in the future.
2 Sally _____ him – don't worry.
3 I _____ the same friends when I leave school because they are going somewhere different.
4 We _____ the coral reefs when we go to Australia. I can't wait!
5 I _____ in Australia when I'm older.
6 _____ Alex _____ at the skatepark? No, he won't.
7 **A** When _____ you _____ learning to surf?
   B I don't know.
8 We usually go on holiday in July, so we _____ at home.

2 **Match questions 1–6 with answers A–F.**
1 **B** What will you do when you get home?
2 ___ Will you go to college when you leave school?
3 ___ Will you see your friends this weekend?
4 ___ When will you see your best friend?
5 ___ Will you go out on your bike on Saturday?
6 ___ Where will you watch TV this evening?

A I don't know. I think I'll see him tomorrow.
B I'll have a snack and do my homework.
C No, I won't. It's too cold to cycle.
D Yes, I will. I want to study English.
E I'll watch it in the living room with my family.
F Yes, I will. We always meet at the café.

3 **Complete the dialogue.**
Ken Where were you? We'll ¹ **be** late for the cinema now.
Zach Sorry, I was at the gym.
Ken OK, well, let's go.
Zach Don't worry, it's just adverts first – we ² _____ miss the film.
Ken Did you ask your mum to come and get us?
Zach Yes, I think she ³ _____ come when she finishes work.
Ken Great! Do you think the film will ⁴ _____ good?
Zach I don't know! ⁵ _____ you leave early?
Ken No, I ⁶ _____!

4 **Match sentence halves 1–8 to A–H.**
1 If you go to Australia, **F**
2 If we take the bus, ___
3 If we go into town, ___
4 He won't go to the party ___
5 I'll go swimming with you ___
6 We'll visit Central Park ___
7 If they don't leave soon, ___
8 You'll upset her ___

A it will be cheaper.   E if you say that.
B they'll be late.   F will you visit Brisbane?
C if we have time.   G will you drive us?
D if the weather's bad!   H if you don't ask him.

5 **Complete the dialogue with the first conditional. Use the correct form of the verbs in brackets and add *if* where necessary.**
Gini If I ¹ **go** (go) for a run, ² **will you come** (you / come) with me?
Meg OK. I ³ _____ (ask) Amy ⁴ _____ (she / want) to come, too.
Gini ⁵ _____ (you / ask) Amy, we ⁶ _____ (have to) run faster.
Meg That's true, she's really quick, and she ⁷ _____ (not wait) for us ⁸ _____ (we / slow).
Gini That's OK. We ⁹ _____ (get) a really fast time ¹⁰ _____ (we / go) with her!
Meg Yes! Let's do it!

6 **Write first conditional sentences.**
1 you not study harder / you not pass all your exams
   If you don't study harder, you won't pass all your exams.
2 we not plant the flowers now / they not grow
3 your garden has lots of wildflowers / it attract insects
4 I open the window / it be too noisy to work in here?
5 we reduce air pollution / we feel healthier
6 there is a lot of snow / we go skiing this winter?
7 you go snorkelling / I not come with you
8 Ben enter the rowing competition / he win

7 **Complete the first conditional sentences so they are true for you.**
If the weather is nice at the weekend, I'll go cycling.
1 If the weather is nice at the weekend, _____.
2 _____, I'll call my friend.
3 If I get invited to a party on Saturday, _____.
4 If I see _____ later, _____.
5 _____, I'll go jogging.
6 _____, we'll go cycling.

111

4 MY GRAMMAR REFERENCE AND PRACTICE

be going to for future plans and intentions

- We can use *be going to* to talk about future plans and intentions.
  I'm going to visit my aunt in hospital this evening.
  'Are they going to meet us for lunch later?' 'Yes, they are.'

- We often use *be going to* with future time phrases, e.g. *tomorrow, next week, tonight, next year.*
  I'm going to cycle to work tomorrow.
  'What are you going to do this summer?' 'I'm going to visit my friends in Kenya.'

- We can also use *be going to* with adverbs of (definite) frequency, e.g. *every day, twice a week, monthly.*
  I'm going to exercise every day.

- We form affirmative sentences with:
  Subject + *am / is / are* + *going to* + infinitive without *to*

Affirmative			
Subject + *be*	*going to*	Infinitive without *to*	
I'm	going to	swim	in the sea.
He's / She's / It's		ride	a horse.
You're / We're / They're		visit	friends.

- We form negative sentences with:
  Subject + *am / is / are* + *not* + *going to* + infinitive without *to*

Negative			
Subject + *be*	*going to*	Infinitive without *to*	
I'm not	going to	drive	to the beach.
He / She / It isn't		come	to the party.
You / We / They aren't		go	to the library.

- We form *yes/no* questions with:
  be + subject + *going to* + infinitive without *to* + ?

Yes/No questions				
be	Subject	*going to*	Infinitive without *to*	
Am	I	going to	travel	around America?
Is	he / she / it			
Are	you / we / they		go	to the party?

- We can answer *yes/no* questions with a short answer.
  'Are you going to donate some money?' 'Yes, I am.'
  'Are they going to volunteer to help?' 'No, they're not.'

- We form *wh-* questions with:
  Question word + *am / is / are* + subject + *going to* + verb

Wh- questions				
Question word	*be*	Subject	*going to*	Verb
Where	am	I	going to	go?
When	is	he / she / it		arrive?
What	are	you / we / they		do?

be going to and *will* for predictions

- We can use both *be going to* and *will* to make predictions about the future.

- We usually use *be going to* when there is some evidence in the present to support the prediction, for example what we can see, hear, smell or feel.
  There isn't a cloud in the sky. It's going to be a lovely day.
  I'm not going to finish. There isn't enough time.

- We usually use *will* to make predictions based on what we believe or know.
  You'll love Australia. It's beautiful.
  He won't come. He never comes to parties.

- We use the infinitive form of the verb without *to* after both *be going to* and *will*.

Affirmative and negative: *be going to*				
	Subject	*be going to*	Infinitive without *to*	
+	It	's going to	rain.	
−	I	'm not going to	win	this race.

Affirmative and negative: *will*				
	Subject	*will / won't*	Infinitive without *to*	
+	You	'll	have	a great time.
−	Sam	won't	be	late.

> **REMEMBER!** We often use *I don't think* with *be going to* or *will* when we are less certain about a prediction:
> *I think people won't / aren't going to drive flying cars in the future.* ✗
> *I don't think people will / are going to drive flying cars in the future.* ✓

112

1 Complete the sentences with the correct form of *be going to* and the verbs in the box.

| do   help   pay   take   not travel   volunteer |
| walk   ~~not watch~~ |

1 Oh no! I **'m not going to watch** this film. Turn it off!
2 We _____ to the shops for our neighbour. She needs some milk and she can't get there.
3 When _____ you _____ your homework?
4 Sara _____ her smartphone back to the shop.
5 _____ you _____ me or not? I can't do this!
6 My mum _____ for a new pair of shoes.
7 _____ Dave _____ at the youth club?
8 They _____ by plane anymore.

2 Choose the correct option.
1 I'm going to _____ my driving test next year.
  A to take   **B** take   C taking
2 _____ going to be at home this weekend?
  A You are   B Is you   C Are you
3 I _____ invite Ula to my party.
  A 's going to   B 'm going to   C 'm go to
4 Tanya isn't going to _____ her seat.
  A offer   B to offer   C to offering
5 _____ going to play football this weekend?
  A Is Ben   B Ben is   C Ben isn't
6 We _____ going to buy a new car this year.
  A not   B isn't   C aren't
7 Which charity _____ donate your money to?
  A are you going to   B you are going to   C you going to
8 Where is Lily _____ next year?
  A study   B going to study   C going study

3 Complete the dialogue with the correct form of the verbs in brackets and *be going to*.
Ben [1] **Are you going to help out** (you / help out) this weekend at the charity book sale?
Lara Yes, I am. I [2] _____ (get) there early so that I can organize the books.
Ben What time [3] _____ (you / arrive)?
Lara At eight o'clock. Do you want to come?
Ben Yes, please.
Lara My mum [4] _____ (take) me. Would you like to come with us?
Ben Thank you. I [5] _____ (not stay) for long because Nick [6] _____ (meet) me to play football.

4 Match sentences 1–6 to A–F.
1 **D** She looks miserable.
2 ___ I'm really hungry.
3 ___ There's a lot of traffic.
4 ___ They practised hard.
5 ___ Don't climb so high.
6 ___ Holly's sorry she hurt your feelings.

A I think I'll order a pizza.
B You're going to fall.
C She won't do it again.
D It looks like she's going to cry.
E They'll win.
F We're going to be late.

5 Choose the best option.
1 That boy is travelling very fast on his bike. He **('s going to)** / **will** have an accident.
2 Katy's usually in the library after school, so I'm sure that I **'ll** / **'m going to** see her later.
3 That smells great – dinner **will** / **'s going to** be delicious!
4 Grandma is planting lots of new flowers. The garden **will** / **'s going to** look really colourful in the summer.
5 Fiona is a very confident person. She **'ll** / **'s going to** meet new people easily.
6 James is quite lazy – he **won't** / **isn't going to** get a job in the summer holidays.

6 Complete the dialogue with *will* or (*be*) *going to* and the correct form of the verbs in brackets.
Mum Look at all the cars. It [1] **'s going to be** (be) busy in town today. I wanted to take these old trousers to the charity shop.
Fin Mum, they only take things they can sell. They [2] _____ (not want) Dad's old trousers.
Mum Yes, they [3] _____ – I've washed them! I took them a pair like this last week.
Fin Dad [4] _____ (not be) pleased. Wait, those are his favourite pair!
Mum Not so loud! He [5] _____ (hear) you. I can hear him in the room next door.
Fin At least tell him, Mum. Anyway, you [6] _____ (be) late. The charity shop closes in 15 minutes!

7 Make predictions about these times. Write true sentences for you.
1 (this evening)
2 (on Saturday morning)
3 (this summer)
4 (a time of your choice)

113

5 MY GRAMMAR REFERENCE AND PRACTICE

can / can't, could / couldn't

- We use *can / can't* to talk about abilities in the present.
  I can ski.
- We use *could* and *couldn't* to talk about abilities in the past.
  My sister could run very fast when she was 12, but she couldn't ride a bike.
- We use an infinitive without *to* after *can / can't* or *could / couldn't*. The forms are the same for all subjects.
  I / He / She / It / You / We / They can / could run 5 km in less than 30 minutes.
- To form questions, we change the order of *can / could* and the subject.
  Can you ride a bike?
  Could you read when you were five?

Present ability	I can ride a bike.
	She can't drive a car.
Questions	Can they cook?
Short answers	Yes, they can. / No, they can't.

Past ability	I could talk when I was two years old.
	They couldn't swim when they were five.
Questions	Could he speak English when he was young?
Short answers	Yes, he could. / No, he couldn't.

- We use *can / can't* or *could / couldn't* to talk about rules.
  You can take a dictionary into the exam.
  We couldn't speak during the exam.
- We also use *can* to make a request or to ask for permission to do something.
  'Can we eat in here?' 'No, you can't.'
  'Can I go to Sarah's party?' 'Yes, you can.'

Present permission	You can drive a car when you're 17.
	We can't go to the party on Friday.
Questions	Can I go to the cinema?
Short answers	Yes, you can. / No, you can't.

Past permission	I could come home at 10 p.m. on Saturday.
	We couldn't use our mobiles at school.
Questions	Could you go into town with your friends?
Short answers	Yes, we could. / No, we couldn't.

REMEMBER! We don't use *do* to form questions with *can / could*:
Do you can / could ride a bike? ✗

Comparative and superlative adverbs

- We use comparative adverbs with *than* to say that a person or group does things better, worse or differently to another person or group.
  The girls play more quietly than the boys.
- For most adverbs ending in *-ly* or *-ily*, we form the comparative with *more*. For adverbs with the same form as the adjective, we add *-er*.

Comparative adverbs		
Adverbs that end in *-ly* or *-ily*	*more* + adverb	quietly → more quietly easily → more easily
Adverbs with the same form as the adjective	add *-er*	fast → faster hard → harder

- Some adverbs have two different comparative forms. The forms ending in *-er* are more informal.
  My sister eats ice cream more quickly / quicker than me.
  Dave works more slowly / slower than Ed.
- Some adverbs are irregular and have an irregular comparative form.

Adjective	Adverb	Comparative adverb
good	well	better
bad	badly	worse

- We use superlative adverbs to compare the way one person does something to the way others (in a group) do it.
  Jenna works the hardest in our office.
- For most adverbs ending in *-ly* or *-ily*, we form the superlative with *the most*. For adverbs with the same form as the adjective, we add *the + -est*.

Superlative adverbs		
Adverbs that end in *-ly* or *-ily*	*the most* + adverb	quietly → the most quietly easily → the most easily
Adverbs with the same form as the adjective	*the + -est*	fast → the fastest hard → the hardest

- Some adverbs have two different superlative forms. The forms ending *-est* are more informal.
  My sister eats ice cream the quickest / most quickly.
  Dave works the slowest / most slowly.
- Some adverbs are irregular and have an irregular superlative form.

Adjective	Adverb	Superlative adverb
good	well	(the) best
bad	badly	(the) worst

1 **Complete the sentences with can / can't or could / couldn't.**
   1 My brother can't ride a bike.
   2 When I was four I _____ read.
   3 My mum _____ speak two languages.
   4 Ali _____ swim, so she's having lessons.
   5 _____ you ski?
   6 I _____ play the guitar when I was young, but I _____ now.
   7 _____ you walk when you were one?
   8 My sister _____ dance really well.

2 **Choose the correct option.**
   1 Can I _____ it now?
      A to eat   (B) eat
   2 No, you _____ use your mobile phone in class.
      A can   B can't
   3 _____ sit in the front seat of the car when you were young?
      A You could   B Could you
   4 My uncle owns the restaurant so I _____ eat for free.
      A can   B could
   5 I'm sorry. You _____ play football here.
      A can't   B couldn't
   6 Excuse me, Mrs Bond, _____ I borrow this?
      A can   B can't
   7 Can I take this book home, please? _____
      A I'm sorry, but you couldn't.
      B I'm sorry, but you can't.

3 **Complete the sentences with can (+) / can't (−) or could (+) / couldn't (−) and the verbs in the box.**

   | eat | play | ride | run | sing | ~~speak~~ | text | walk |

   1 My dad could speak French when he was young, but can't now! (+)
   2 Tilly _____ a bike until she was seven. (−)
   3 I _____ lots of different card games. (+)
   4 _____ I _____ to school on my own please, Mum?
   5 A _____ you _____ ?
      B Yes, I can. Do you want to hear?
   6 You _____ your friends in class. (−)
   7 My mum _____ 10 km in 45 minutes when she was 30. (+)
   8 We _____ sweets at school when we were younger. (−)

4 **Write sentences, questions and short answers with can / can't or could / couldn't.**
   1 in the UK / you / get a job / when you're 13
      In the UK, you can get a job when you're 13.
   2 A your sister / drive?
      B No, / she
   3 in 1990 / teenagers / leave school / when they were 16
   4 we / not wear / trainers / at school
   5 you / not watch / this film – it's rated 15
   6 my gran / not use / a computer / when she was at school

5 **Complete the sentences with the correct comparative adverb form of the adjective in brackets.**
   1 Do it more carefully (careful) next time.
   2 Can we walk _____ (slow), please?
   3 Rosy works _____ (hard) than Dora.
   4 He's playing much _____ (bad) than he did yesterday.
   5 Go _____ (fast)!
   6 You need to do _____ (good) than that!
   7 I usually get up _____ (late) at the weekend than during the week.
   8 Heather eats _____ (quick) than the rest of us.

6 **Write sentences with superlative adverbs.**
   1 Who / speak / well / English?
      Who speaks the best English?
   2 I / sleep / quiet / in my family
   3 Jade / run / fast / out of my friends
   4 Joseph / work / hard / in our class
   5 Isla / dance / beautiful / in the show
   6 Ariana always / arrive at hockey practice / late

7 **Complete the sentences with the correct comparative or superlative adverb form of the adjective in brackets.**
   1 My mum makes the best cakes. (good)
   2 You need to check your work _____. (careful)
   3 I play chess _____ my friend Jay. (good)
   4 He began to speak _____ when he saw she couldn't understand. (slow)
   5 Eldon lives _____ to school in our class. (near)
   6 Rob always arrives to class _____ out of all the class. (late)
   7 My brother always argues _____ in the family when we play board games! (loud)
   8 She forgets things now _____ than when she was younger. (easy)

115

6 MY GRAMMAR REFERENCE AND PRACTICE

Present perfect

- We can use the present perfect to talk about life experiences or states that are still relevant in the present.
  Maria has travelled around the world.

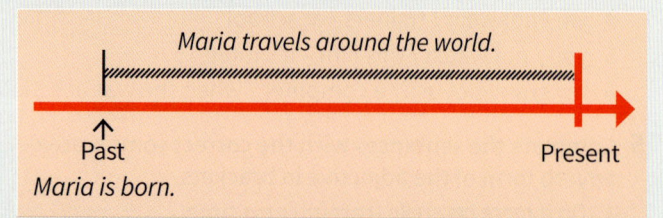

  Maria travels around the world.

  Past — Present
  Maria is born.

- We don't say when the action happened with the present perfect.
  I've visited Paris. (NOT: ~~I've visited Paris last year.~~)

- To say when an action happened in the past, we use the past simple.
  I visited Paris last year.

- We don't use the present perfect to talk about the experiences of dead people.
  Shakespeare wrote more than 30 plays.
      (NOT: ~~Shakespeare has written more than 30 plays.~~)

- Regular verbs have past participles which are the same as their past simple forms, ending in *-ed*.
  visit, visited → visited   arrive, arrived → arrived

- Irregular verbs have irregular past participles. Sometimes the past participle of an irregular verb is the same as the past simple form and sometimes it is different.
  do, did → done   have, had → had
  eat, ate → eaten   lose, lost → lost

- We form present perfect simple affirmative with:
  Subject + *have* / *has* + past participle

Affirmative			
Subject	have / has	Past participle	
I / You / We / They	have	played	in a band.
He / She / It	has	had	dance lessons.

- We form the present perfect simple negative with:
  Subject + *haven't* / *hasn't* + past participle

Negative			
Subject	haven't / hasn't	Past participle	
I / You / We / They	haven't	played	basketball.
He / She / It	hasn't	had	swimming lessons.

- We form present perfect *yes/no* questions with:
  Have / *Has* + subject + past participle

Questions			
Have / Has	Subject	Past participle	
Have	I / you / we / they	played	in a team?
Has	he / she / it	had	any injuries?

- We form short answers with:
  Yes / *No* + subject + *have* / *haven't* or *has* / *hasn't*
  'Have you done your homework?' 'Yes, I have.'
  'Has Jane seen Kylie?' 'No, she hasn't.'
  There has / *have been* is the present perfect form of *there is* / *are*.
  There has been a lot of noise.
  There haven't been any problems.

Present perfect with *ever* and *never*

- We can use *ever* and *never* when we talk about life experiences up to now.

- *Ever* means 'at any time in the past'. We use it in questions.
  Have you ever climbed a mountain?
  Has she ever worked in a restaurant before?

- *Never* means 'at no time in the past'. We use it with an affirmative verb.
  I've never read The Goblet of Fire.
  He's never been to China.

> **REMEMBER!** We don't use *not* and *never* together:
> *I haven't never watched a horror film.* ✗
> *I've never watched a horror film.* ✓

1 Write the past participles of the verbs.
1 walk *walked*
2 try _____
3 win _____
4 run _____
5 find _____
6 write _____
7 stop _____
8 give _____
9 catch _____
10 enjoy _____
11 do _____
12 see _____

2 Choose the correct option.
1 Peter **have** / (**has**) been to Egypt.
2 We **haven't** / **hasn't** seen your bag.
3 I **given** / **'ve given** them some food.
4 **Have** / **Has** you tried this?
5 You **aren't** / **haven't** cleaned your teeth.
6 **Have** / **Has** the children done their homework?
7 Anna has **watch** / **watched** that film twice.
8 **A** Have you had dinner?
  B No, we **haven't** / **hasn't**.
9 Have **read you** / **you read** those emails?

3 Find the mistake. Write the correct present perfect sentence.
1 We're visited Frankfurt and Berlin.
  We've visited Frankfurt and Berlin.
2 You read this book?
  _____
3 We hadn't a holiday this year.
  _____
4 The team haven't did enough strength training.
  _____
5 Mandy isn't found a job.
  _____
6 Who has took my bike?
  _____
7 I hasn't heard the news.
  _____
8 He did washed the car.
  _____

4 Complete the sentences with the correct form of the present perfect simple and the verbs in the box.

not finish   lose   start   ~~try~~   win   not work

1 I've never *tried* spinach.
2 Lou _____ yoga and she loves it.
3 I _____ at the shop for long.
4 _____ he _____ a lot of weight?
5 Wait for me! I'm watching the game and it _____.
6 _____ they _____ the match?

5 Write present perfect simple sentences with *ever* or *never*.
1 I / have / acting lessons
  I've never had acting lessons.
2 you / injure / yourself / ?
3 we / work out / at an outdoor gym
4 you / meet / a famous sportsperson / ?
5 I / win / a race
6 Nadia / try / yoga before
7 I / forget / to send you a birthday card / ?

6 Write present perfect questions for the answers.
1 **A** *Have you ever been to Canada?* (go / Canada)
  B No, I've never been to Canada. But I'd like to go.
2 **A** _____ ?
  (win / money)
  B No, but I'd love to win some money one day.
3 **A** _____ ?
  (see / a lion)
  B Yes, I saw a lion when I was on holiday in South Africa.
4 **A** _____ ?
  (run / 5 km)
  B Yes, I ran 5 km yesterday and I did it in 26 minutes!
5 **A** _____ ?
  (use / a fitness app)
  B Yes, I often use a fitness app to do strength training.
6 **A** _____ ?
  (swim / 2 km)
  B No, I haven't. I'm not a good swimmer – 2 km is too far for me!

7 Complete the dialogue with *have* or *haven't* and the correct form of the verbs in brackets.
Hiro ¹*Have you ever gone* (you / go) swimming in a lake or river?
Sam No, I ² _____. Have you?
Hiro Yes, I ³ _____.
Sam Where ⁴ _____ (you / do) it?
Hiro There's a lake near my house.
  I ⁵ _____ (be) in there a few times, but I'm not sure I like it anymore.
Sam Why not?
Hiro Well, I ⁶ _____ (not / see) any fish yet, but I'm sure they're down there. The water's very dark.
Sam Hmm. ⁷ _____ (you ever / feel) a fish swimming about?
Hiro Yes, I ⁸ _____. Well, I think so.
Sam Ha ha! ⁹ _____ (you ever / see) the film *Jaws*?
Hiro Very funny. Sharks live in the sea.
Sam Well, stranger things ¹⁰ _____ (happen)! You never know.
Hiro Hmm …

117

7 MY GRAMMAR REFERENCE AND PRACTICE

should / shouldn't, must / mustn't

should / shouldn't

- We use *should / shouldn't* to give advice and ask for advice.
  Your cough sounds bad. You should see a doctor.
  You shouldn't study for too long without a break.
  'Should I invite Julio to the cinema?'
  'Yes, you should.' / 'No, you shouldn't.'

- We use an infinitive without *to* after *should / shouldn't*.
  You should do more exercise. (NOT: *You should to do more exercise.*)

Affirmative and negative				
Subject	should	Infinitive without *to*	
I / He / She / It / You / We / They	should	go	home.
	shouldn't	wear	a coat.

- To form *yes/no* questions, we change the order of *should* and the subject.
  Should she exercise more?

- We often use short answers with questions that begin with *should*.
  'Should I go now?' 'Yes, you should.' / 'No, you shouldn't.'

- We can also form questions with a question word:
  Question word + *should* + subject + infinitive without *to* + ?
  What should we wear to the party?

must / mustn't

- We use *must* to talk about what is necessary to do (obligation).
  You must finish all your homework.

- We use *must not* or *mustn't* to talk about what is prohibited or against the rules.
  Students must not use mobile phones in class.
  You mustn't tell Sarah – it's a secret.

- We usually form questions with *have to* rather than *must*.
  'Do I have to do all the exercises?' 'Yes, you do.'

- We use an infinitive without *to* after *must*.
  I must eat more fruit. (NOT: *I must to eat more fruit.*)

- The form of *must* is the same for every subject (*I, you, it, they*, etc.).

- To form the negative, we use *must not* (*mustn't*):
  Subject + *must not* (*mustn't*) + infinitive without *to*

Affirmative and negative			
Subject	must	Infinitive without *to*	
I / He / She / It / You / We / They	must	finish	all your homework.
	must not / mustn't	tell	Sarah.

have (got) to + infinitive without *to*

- We use *have (got) to* to talk about what is necessary.
  All students have to study a foreign language.
  He has got to call his sister.

- We use *don't / doesn't have to* or *haven't / hasn't got to* when there is a choice (it isn't necessary).
  I don't have to / haven't got to get up early tomorrow.

Affirmative and negative			
Subject	have to	Infinitive without *to*	
I / He / She / It / You / We / They	have to / have got to	get up	early.
	don't have to / haven't got to	leave	yet.

> **REMEMBER!** We don't use short forms with *have to*:
> *I've to call my dad.* ✗
> *I have to call my dad.* ✓
> But we can use short forms with *have got to*:
> *I've got to call my dad.* ✓

- We use *do / does* to form *have to* questions.
  Do / Does + subject + *have to* + infinitive without *to* + ?
  Does he have to do this exercise?

- Or we use *have / has* to form *have got to* questions.
  Have / Has + subject + *got to* + infinitive without *to* + ?
  Have we got to leave now?

- We often give short answers to questions with *have to* or *have got to*.
  'Do I have to go to London tomorrow?' 'No, you don't.'
  'Has he got to wait for them?' 'Yes, he has.'

118

1 **Complete the sentences with *should* or *shouldn't*.**
   1 You *shouldn't* eat a lot of fast food.
   2 You _____ walk to work.
   3 You _____ look at a computer all day.
   4 You _____ brush your teeth every day.
   5 You _____ eat fruit and vegetables.
   6 You _____ sit at a desk all day.
   7 You _____ drink a lot of coffee.
   8 You _____ get eight hours of sleep.

2 **Complete the second line of text so that it means the same as the first. Use *should* or *shouldn't* in your answer.**
   1 We're bored! It would be good fun to go to the beach!
     We *should go to the beach*.
   2 You spend so much money on clothes. It's not good.
     You _____ so much money on clothes.
   3 I'm thinking of painting the walls. What colour do you think?
     What colour _____ ?
   4 In my opinion, joining the tennis club would be really good for you. Do it!
     You _____ club.
   5 It's Elena's birthday today. How about we make a cake for her?
     _____ a cake for Elena's birthday?
   6 In my opinion, sitting on the teacher's chair isn't a good idea. Don't do it!
     You _____ on the teacher's chair.
   7 I could stay or I could go. What do you think?
     _____ go?

3 **Match instructions 1–8 to people A–H.**
   1 *E* You must have lights on your bike at night.
   2 ___ You must tidy your bedroom.
   3 ___ You must eat more fruit and vegetables.
   4 ___ You must try to run faster.
   5 ___ You must sit down in your seat when we're moving.
   6 ___ You mustn't take photos in here.
   7 ___ You mustn't touch these chemicals.
   8 ___ You mustn't eat so many sweets.

   A sports teacher
   B parent
   C museum guide
   D dentist
   E police officer
   F doctor
   G bus driver
   H science teacher

4 **Write rules for the library and the swimming pool. Use *must / mustn't* and the words in the box.**

   | ~~be quiet~~ bring pets eat or drink have a shower |
   | jump return books run wear |

   The library
   1 *You must be quiet in the library.*
   2 _____
   3 _____
   4 _____

   The swimming pool
   1 _____
   2 _____
   3 _____
   4 _____

5 **Complete the sentences with *have / has (got) to* and the verbs in brackets.**
   1 Tim can't come out this evening. He *has to finish* his project. (finish)
   2 I can't stay. I _____ in half an hour. (go)
   3 You _____ to visit museums in the UK – they're free. (pay)
   4 Kate _____ glasses. She can see very well. (wear)
   5 You _____ me with my homework. I've finished it. (help)
   6 Does your mum _____ at the weekend? (work)
   7 You _____ about the party now. Let me know tomorrow. (decide)
   8 What do we _____ for our homework? (do)

6 **Write sentences with the correct form of *have (got) to*.**
   1 I / not / go to bed early / at the weekend
     I don't have to/haven't got to go to bed early at the weekend.
   2 Kay / practise / the piano / every day
   3 they / see / the head teacher / at lunchtime
   4 you / do / homework / every night?
   5 we / not / wear / a uniform for school
   6 he / work / at the weekend?

7 **Complete the sentences for you.**
   Give yourself two pieces of advice:
   I should _____.
   I shouldn't _____.
   Write what you must and mustn't do today:
   I must _____.
   I mustn't _____.
   Write what you have to and don't have to do this week:
   I have to _____.
   I don't have to _____.

119

8 MY GRAMMAR REFERENCE AND PRACTICE

Reflexive pronouns

- Reflexive pronouns all end in *-self* or *-selves*. We use them when the subject is also the object of the verb in a sentence.

  Martin *is teaching* himself *Chinese.* (= Martin is teaching Martin (himself) Chinese.)

Subject	Verb	Reflexive pronoun
I	hurt	myself.
You		yourself.
He		himself.
She		herself.
It		itself.
We		ourselves.
You		yourselves.
They		themselves.

- Reflexive pronouns often appear after these verbs:

  admire   behave   cut   dry   enjoy   hate
  help   hurt   introduce   love   prepare   teach

- Some verb + reflexive pronoun combinations have a particular meaning:

  The children always behave themselves. (= They always behave well.)
  I really enjoyed myself. (= I had a good time.)
  Help yourself to some more cake. (= Take some more cake if you want some.)

- Reflexive pronouns don't always follow a verb. They can also be the object of a preposition.

  Sam made a sandwich for himself.

- We can use reflexive pronouns *yourself* / *yourselves* with the imperative form (without a subject) to wish good things for people.

  Look after yourself!
  Enjoy yourselves at the party!

- We can also use reflexive pronouns to mean 'without help'.

  I did it (all by) myself. (= I did it without help.)

Indefinite pronouns

- We use *somebody* / *someone*, *something* or *somewhere* in affirmative sentences to talk about a person, thing or place when we can't (or don't want to) be specific about what we are talking about.

- We use *somebody* / *someone*, *something* or *somewhere* in affirmative sentences.

  Somebody sent you a birthday card.
     (= I don't know who sent it.)

- We can also use *some-* indefinite pronouns in questions that are offers or requests.

  Would you like something to drink?
  Will somebody come with me?

- We usually use *anybody* / *anyone*, *anything* and *anywhere* in negative sentences and questions.

  I don't know anyone in my class.
  Is there anywhere to buy a sandwich near here?

	One	None (negatives / questions)
People	somebody / someone	anybody / anyone
Things	something	anything
Places	somewhere	anywhere

- The endings *-body* and *-one* have the same meaning.

Question tags

- We use question tags to check information or to find out if someone agrees with us. A statement with a question tag often seems more polite than a direct question or plain statement.

  This is the quickest way to your house, isn't it?
     (checking information)
  The film was awful, wasn't it? (asking for agreement)

- When the main verb is affirmative, the question tag is negative and when the main verb is negative, the question tag is affirmative.

  You were *on holiday,* weren't *you?*
  You weren't *happy,* were *you?*

- When the statement contains an auxiliary verb (*be*, *have*, *do*) or a modal verb (e.g. *can*, *will*, *should*), repeat it in the question tag.

  We aren't *going to be late,* are *we?*
  You can *skateboard,* can't *you?*

- When there isn't an auxiliary or modal verb in the statement, we use the correct form of *do* in the question tag.

  You moved here from Spain, didn't *you?*

	Statement	Question tag
Present simple	You like walking,	don't you?
Present perfect	You haven't seen my bag,	have you?
Past simple	It was your last day yesterday,	wasn't it?
will	You'll find me,	won't you?
can	We can't meet,	can we?
should	We shouldn't do this,	should we?

120

1 Match sentence halves 1–7 to A–G.
1 I'd like to have a car that drives B
2 It's OK. I haven't hurt _____
3 We didn't get any help. We did it all by _____
4 Jack! Are you talking to _____
5 She bought a coffee for _____
6 The girls baked the cake _____
7 Did you two paint the room _____

A yourself?
B itself.
C ourselves.
D yourselves?
E myself.
F themselves.
G herself.

2 Complete the sentences with the words in the box.

| her   herself   himself   myself   ourselves |
| themselves   us   ~~yourself~~ |

1 Did you teach *yourself* the guitar?
2 My grandmother looks after _____ – she's very fit and healthy.
3 The restaurant manager is a friend, so he gives _____ a discount when we eat there. It's very nice of him.
4 It's true, they're cycling across Europe. They told me _____ .
5 She fell and broke _____ leg.
6 He isn't enjoying _____ today.
7 I bought _____ a new bike yesterday.
8 We enjoyed _____ at the party.

3 Choose the correct option.
1 I didn't break **something** / **(anything)**.
2 Shall we go **somewhere** / **anywhere** nice on your birthday?
3 Waiter, there's **something** / **someone** in my soup. I think it's an insect.
4 We didn't do **something** / **anything** yesterday.
5 'I'm texting **someone** / **anyone** from school.' 'Oh, who? Do I know them?'
6 Put the money **somewhere** / **anywhere** safe.
7 We heard a noise from the garden, but we can't see **somebody** / **anybody** out there.
8 I'm not going **somewhere** / **anywhere** in a plane. I'm scared of flying!

4 Complete the sentences with the correct indefinite pronouns.
1 I'd like to go *somewhere* hot and sunny.
2 Let's do _____ educational in the holidays.
3 We didn't do _____ except lie on the beach all day.
4 Has _____ seen my sunglasses?
5 I don't want to go to the usual tourist sites. I want to go _____ completely different.
6 I like holidays with my family, but I prefer going with _____ else.

5 Complete the text with the correct reflexive or indefinite pronouns.

The first time that I went on holiday by ¹*myself* (at least, without my parents) abroad was when I was 18. My friend, Nicola, and I wanted to enjoy ² _____ somewhere fun, warm and sunny. So, we went to the Greek island of Rhodes. It was amazing! ³ _____ can borrow a motorbike for a few days, so we travelled ⁴ _____ on that little bike. We visited some very busy towns, but also some small quiet villages where there was ⁵ _____ around – maybe just a cat or dog. We also went on a boat trip. Nicola enjoyed ⁶ _____ swimming in the beautiful deep blue water, but I was happy doing ⁷ _____ except relaxing on the boat. The Greek Islands are magical, so what are you waiting for? Buy ⁸ _____ a ticket and go!

6 Match question halves 1–8 to A–H.
1 It's been a long hard day, C
2 They didn't receive your email, _____
3 Mia will be at the party, _____
4 Filip doesn't enjoy camping, _____
5 You can't repair that, _____
6 She won't agree with us, _____
7 It hasn't rained all day, _____
8 We should organize a party, _____

A can you?
B won't she?
C hasn't it?
D shouldn't we?
E did they?
F has it?
G does he?
H will she?

7 Complete the questions with question tags.
1 You won't tell anyone, *will you*?
2 You can drive, _____ ?
3 I've really improved, _____ ?
4 We didn't spend enough time on the beach, _____ ?
5 Ben can borrow your phone, _____ ?
6 We should go back to France next year, _____ ?
7 She'll work hard, _____ ?
8 You felt OK, _____ ?

121

1 CULTURE 360° AN EGYPTIAN TOMB

LESSON OBJECTIVES
- Learn about communication in Ancient Egypt
- Talk about historical tombs

THINK

1 Look at the photo of Ramses the Sixth's tomb in Egypt. What can you see?

EXPLORE

Access the interactive 360° content now!

2 Look at the timeline of Ancient Egypt and answer the questions.
1 Which three things or people below came from Egypt?

Rulers	Cleopatra	Julius Caesar	King Arthur
Writing systems	Cuneiform	Hieroglyphics	Sanskrit
Buildings	The Colosseum	The Parthenon	The pyramids of Giza

2 Did Cleopatra rule Egypt before or after Ramses the Sixth?

3 Read about Ramses the Sixth's tomb. Match the words 1–4 to their meanings A–D.
1 .... pharaoh
2 .... valley
3 .... sarcophagus
4 .... treasure

A a low area of land between mountains or hills
B a decorated stone coffin
C a king
D valuable items, e.g. gold coins or jewellery

4 Listen to an expert talking about hieroglyphics. Answer the questions.
1 What did the symbols represent?
2 Which direction did they write hieroglyphics in?
3 Where did the Egyptians write hieroglyphics?
4 When did scribes start to learn how to write hieroglyphics?

5 Look at the hieroglyphic alphabet. Then translate the hieroglyphic message below into English, from left to right. Watch out! Some different letters have the same symbol.

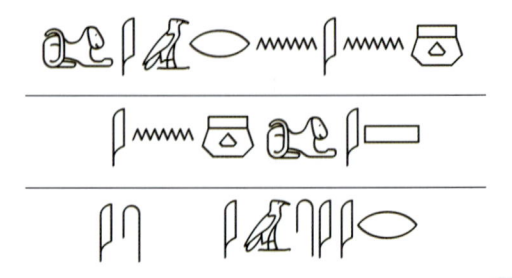

REFLECT ON CULTURE

6 Discuss the questions in pairs.
1 Can you think of any famous historical tombs in your country?
2 Do you think historical tombs should be opened or kept closed?

Look UP! Look online and find out:
Which animal did the Egyptians think was special and brought good luck?

2 CULTURE 360° HANBURY STREET, LONDON

LESSON OBJECTIVES
- Learn about life as a street artist
- Talk about street art

THINK

1 Look at the photo of a street in London. Answer the questions.
1. What can you see in the photo?
2. Are there any examples of street art near you?
3. Do you think street art is important? Why / Why not?

EXPLORE

Access the interactive 360° content now!

2 Watch the video. Are the sentences true (T) or false (F)?
1. It's easy to find walls to paint. _____
2. Street artists haven't got a lot of free time. _____
3. Street artists often become famous quickly. _____

3 Watch the video. Which adjective describes the artist's feelings when someone paints over his work?

| disappointed | excited | scared | surprised |

4 Read the social media posts. Answer the questions about street artists.
1. Why did Roa change his painting from a crane to a heron?
2. Why does Dingo think street artists shouldn't show their work on social media?
3. How can social media help street artists?

5 How is life as a street artist different to other artists? Think about:
- finding places to work
- their social life
- protecting their work
- the law
- making money

REFLECT ON CULTURE

6 What skills or personal qualities do you think make a good street artist?

Look UP! Look online and find out about Roa, the street artist:
Where is he from?
What does he paint?
Where can you see his art?

3 CULTURE 360° GAMES CAFÉ

LESSON OBJECTIVES
- Discover what we can learn from games
- Talk about games in your country

THINK

1 Look at the photo of a games café. What games can you see on the tables? Would you like to visit this place? Why / Why not?

EXPLORE

🔊 ▶ Access the interactive 360° content now!

2 ⬥ Watch the video of Gemma and Leo. Complete the texts.

THE PLAYERS

Gemma often meets her friends in the café on ¹_____. She ² _____ plays Jenga or Taboo. She can't stand ³_____ games because she thinks they're ⁴_____.

Leo is ⁵_____ about Uno because he always wins. He ⁶_____ plays Catan. He's very good at planning. He ⁷_____ often play Taboo because his friends don't like it.

3 ⬤ Watch the video about the games below. What skills do they need? Match the games 1–4 to skills A–D.

GAMES
1. Catan
2. Taboo
3. Jenga
4. Uno

SKILLS
- A Matching
- B Languages
- C Hand-eye coordination
- D Planning

4 ★ Watch the video animation. In pairs, play Taboo.

REFLECT ON CULTURE

5 What are the traditional games in your country? Are they an important part of your country's culture?

Look UP! Look online and find out:
What are the most popular board games or card games in your country?

4 CULTURE 360° PROP-MAKER'S WORKSHOP

LESSON OBJECTIVES
- Learn about film props
- Talk about working in films

THINK

1 Read the description below. How many film, theatre or TV props can you think of that are special and help to tell the story?

> **Props** are objects that actors use in films, theatre or TV programmes. These can be common things, like books or plants, that make the environment look real. Some props are special objects that are important to the story.

EXPLORE

Access the interactive 360° content now!

2 Explore the 360° photo of a prop-maker's workshop. Find these props in the workshop.
- a fossil
- a space weapon
- a train
- a trophy
- a uniform
- a white hat
- jewellery
- some old books

3 Watch the video. Answer the questions.
1 What type of film is the prop-maker working on? Choose from A–F.
  - A an historical drama
  - B a science fiction film
  - C a western
  - D an action adventure
  - E a war film
  - F a superhero film
2 What prop is she designing?

4 Watch the video. Answer the questions.
1 What type of props does the prop-maker design?
2 Why do the props need to look real?
3 How does he make the props?

5 Watch the video. Discuss the questions in pairs.
1 Do you think this is a good job? Why / Why not?
2 What skills do you think you need to make jewellery for films?
3 What other jobs can people do in films?

REFLECT ON CULTURE

6 Think about your favourite film. What props can you remember from the film? Make a list. Then choose three props from your list and write a sentence about each one. Explain why the prop is important for the film.

Look UP! Look online and find out:
Were any famous films made in your country?
Are any film props made in your country?

125

5 CULTURE 360° — UROS FLOATING ISLANDS, PERU

LESSON OBJECTIVES
- Explore a popular tourist destination
- Talk about the effects of tourism

THINK

1 Look at the photo of the floating islands of Uros in Peru. What can you see? How do you think tourism affects a place like this?

EXPLORE

Access the interactive 360° content now!

2 Watch the video. Answer the questions.
   1 How do tourists get to the islands?
   2 Where do the locals get most of their money from?
   3 What materials do the locals use to make their souvenirs?

3 Listen to the conversation between two tourists on one of the islands. Choose the correct option.
   1 The man wants to visit the **houses** / **boats** on the island.
   2 The man and woman **agree** / **disagree**.
   3 The man wants to **learn about the culture** / **take photos** of the island.

4 Listen to the tour guide. How is life on the islands different today compared to the past? Do you think this is a positive change for the people who live there?

5 Watch the slideshow. According to the online posts, which of these activities can tourists do on Uros?

- [ ] Stay in local accommodation
- [ ] Make hot water bottles
- [ ] Dress up in traditional local clothes
- [ ] Make 'totora' grass floors
- [ ] Buy local products
- [ ] Make souvenir grass boats

REFLECT ON CULTURE

6 Think again about your answer to exercise 1. What are the positive and negative effects that tourism can have on a place?

Look UP! Look online and find out:
Where is Lake Titicaca?
Find two interesting facts about the lake or its islands.

IRREGULAR VERB LIST

Infinitive		Past simple		Past participle	
be	/biː/	was / were	/wɒz/, /wɜː(r)/	been	/biːn/
beat	/biːt/	beat	/biːt/	beaten	/biːtn/
become	/bɪˈkʌm/	became	/bɪˈkeɪm/	become	/bɪˈkʌm/
begin	/bɪˈɡɪn/	began	/bɪˈɡæn/	begun	/bɪˈɡʌn/
bite	/baɪt/	bit	/bɪt/	bitten	/bɪtn/
blow	/bləʊ/	blew	/bluː/	blown	/bləʊn/
break	/breɪk/	broke	/brəʊk/	broken	/ˈbrəʊkən/
bring	/brɪŋ/	brought	/brɔːt/	brought	/brɔːt/
burn	/bɜːn/	burnt / burned	/bɜːnt/, /bɜːnd/	burnt / burned	/bɜːnt/, /bɜːnd/
build	/bɪld/	built	/bɪlt/	built	/bɪlt/
buy	/baɪ/	bought	/bɔːt/	bought	/bɔːt/
can	/kæn/	could	/kəd/		
catch	/kætʃ/	caught	/kɔːt/	caught	/kɔːt/
choose	/tʃuːz/	chose	/tʃəʊz/	chosen	/tʃəʊzn/
come	/kʌm/	came	/keɪm/	come	/kʌm/
cost	/kɒst/	cost	/kɒst/	cost	/kɒst/
cut	/kʌt/	cut	/kʌt/	cut	/kʌt/
do	/duː/	did	/dɪd/	done	/dʌn/
draw	/drɔː/	drew	/druː/	drawn	/drɔːn/
dream	/driːm/	dreamt / dreamed	/dremt/, /driːmd/	dreamt / dreamed	/dremt/, /driːmd/
drink	/drɪŋk/	drank	/dræŋk/	drunk	/drʌŋk/
drive	/draɪv/	drove	/drəʊv/	driven	/ˈdrɪvn/
eat	/iːt/	ate	/eɪt/, /et/	eaten	/ˈiːtn/
fall	/fɔːl/	fell	/fel/	fallen	/ˈfɔːlən/
feed	/fiːd/	fed	/fed/	fed	/fed/
feel	/fiːl/	felt	/felt/	felt	/felt/
fight	/faɪt/	fought	/fɔːt/	fought	/fɔːt/
find	/faɪnd/	found	/faʊnd/	found	/faʊnd/
fly	/flaɪ/	flew	/fluː/	flown	/fləʊn/
forget	/fəˈget/	forgot	/fəˈɡɒt/	forgotten	/fəˈɡɒtn/
forgive	/fəˈɡɪv/	forgave	/fəˈɡeɪv/	forgiven	/fəˈɡɪvn/
freeze	/friːz/	froze	/frəʊz/	frozen	/ˈfrəʊzn/
get	/get/	got	/ɡɒt/	got	/ɡɒt/
give	/ɡɪv/	gave	/ɡeɪv/	given	/ˈɡɪvn/
go	/ɡəʊ/	went	/went/	gone / been	/ɡɒn/, /biːn/
grow	/ɡrəʊ/	grew	/ɡruː/	grown	/ɡrəʊn/
hang	/hæŋ/	hung	/hʌŋ/	hung	/hʌŋ/
have	/hæv/	had	/hæd/	had	/hæd/
hear	/hɪə(r)/	heard	/hɜːd/	heard	/hɜːd/
hide	/haɪd/	hid	/hɪd/	hidden	/ˈhɪdn/
hit	/hɪt/	hit	/hɪt/	hit	/hɪt/
hold	/həʊld/	held	/held/	held	/held/
hurt	/hɜːt/	hurt	/hɜːt/	hurt	/hɜːt/
keep	/kiːp/	kept	/kept/	kept	/kept/

IRREGULAR VERB LIST continued

Infinitive		Past simple		Past participle	
know	/nəʊ/	knew	/njuː/	known	/nəʊn/
lead	/liːd/	led	/led/	led	/led/
learn	/lɜːn/	learnt / learned	/lɜːnt /, /lɜːnd/	learnt / learned	/lɜːnt/, /lɜːnd/
leave	/liːv/	left	/left/	left	/left/
lend	/lend/	lent	/lent/	lent	/lent/
let	/let/	let	/let/	let	/let/
lie	/laɪ/	lay	/leɪ/	lain	/leɪn/
lose	/luːz/	lost	/lɒst/	lost	/lɒst/
make	/meɪk/	made	/meɪd/	made	/meɪd/
meet	/miːt/	met	/met/	met	/met/
pay	/peɪ/	paid	/peɪd/	paid	/peɪd/
put	/pʊt/	put	/pʊt/	put	/pʊt/
read	/riːd/	read	/red/	read	/red/
ride	/raɪd/	rode	/rəʊd/	ridden	/ˈrɪdn/
ring	/rɪŋ/	rang	/ræŋ/	rung	/rʌŋ/
run	/rʌn/	ran	/ræn/	run	/rʌn/
say	/seɪ/	said	/sed/	said	/sed/
see	/siː/	saw	/sɔː/	seen	/siːn/
sell	/sel/	sold	/səʊld/	sold	/səʊld/
send	/send/	sent	/sent/	sent	/sent/
set	/set/	set	/set/	set	/set/
shake	/ʃeɪk/	shook	/ʃʊk/	shaken	/ʃeɪkən/
shine	/ʃaɪn/	shone	/ʃɒn/	shone	/ʃɒn/
show	/ʃəʊ/	showed	/ʃəʊd/	shown	/ʃəʊn/
shut	/ʃʌt/	shut	/ʃʌt/	shut	/ʃʌt/
sing	/sɪŋ/	sang	/sæŋ/	sung	/sʌŋ/
sit	/sɪt/	sat	/sæt/	sat	/sæt/
sleep	/sliːp/	slept	/slept/	slept	/slept/
speak	/spiːk/	spoke	/spəʊk/	spoken	/ˈspəʊkən/
spell	/spel/	spelt / spelled	/spelt/, /speld/	spelt / spelled	/spelt/, /speld/
spend	/spend/	spent	/spent/	spent	/spent/
stand	/stænd/	stood	/stʊd/	stood	/stʊd/
steal	/stiːl/	stole	/stəʊl/	stolen	/ˈstəʊlən/
swim	/swɪm/	swam	/swæm/	swum	/swʌm/
take	/teɪk/	took	/tʊk/	taken	/ˈteɪkən/
teach	/tiːtʃ/	taught	/tɔːt/	taught	/tɔːt/
tell	/tel/	told	/təʊld/	told	/təʊld/
think	/θɪŋk/	thought	/θɔːt/	thought	/θɔːt/
throw	/θrəʊ/	threw	/θruː/	thrown	/θrəʊn/
understand	/ˌʌndəˈstænd/	understood	/ˌʌndəˈstʊd/	understood	/ˌʌndəˈstʊd/
wake	/weɪk/	woke	/wəʊk/	woken	/ˈwəʊkən/
wear	/weə(r)/	wore	/wɔː(r)/	worn	/wɔːn/
win	/wɪn/	won	/wʌn/	won	/wʌn/
write	/raɪt/	wrote	/rəʊt/	written	/ˈrɪtn/